*Commonwealth
and Enterprise Paper No. 1*

1999

SME Exports and Public Policies in Mauritius

Ganeshan Wignaraja and Sue O'Neil

Commonwealth Secretariat
The Commonwealth Secretariat is an inter-governmental organisation serving 54 member states which is headquartered in London. **The Export and Industrial Development Division** (EIDD) is a specialised department whose mission is to create competitive enterprise. EIDD provides consultancy and advisory services to member governments in the areas of export promotion, industrial and competitiveness strategy, small business development and agricultural management.

Ganeshan Wignaraja is Chief Programme Officer in the Export and Industrial Development Division of the Commonwealth Secretariat. He is a co-author of a related study *Mauritius: Dynamising Export Competitiveness, Commonwealth Secretariat: London (Commonwealth Economic Papers, No. 33), 1998* (with Sanjaya Lall).

Sue O'Neil is Senior Lecturer in Marketing and Design Management at the Harrow Business School of the University of Westminster.

Commonwealth Secretariat
Marlborough House
Pall Mall, London SW1Y 5HX, United Kingdom

© Commonwealth Secretariat, August 1999

All rights reserved. No part of this publication may be reproduced, stored in a retrieval system, or transmitted in any form or by any means, electronic or mechanical, including photocopying, recording or otherwise without the permission of the publisher.

The authors have asserted their moral rights to be identified as authors of this work

The views expressed in this document do not necessarily reflect the opinion or policy of the Commonwealth Secretariat.

Published by the Commonwealth Secretariat
Designed by bluefrog
Printed in the United Kingdom by Abacus Direct
Wherever possible, the Commonwealth Secretariat uses paper sourced from sustainable forests or from sources that minimise a destructive impact on the environment.

Copies of this publication can be ordered direct from:
Vale Packaging Ltd, 420 Vale Road, Tonbridge, Kent TN9 1TD, United Kingdom
Tel: + 44 (0)1732 359387 Fax: +44 (0) 1732 770620 e-mail: vale@vale-ltd.co.uk

Price: £8.50   ISBN: 0-85092-620-3

Web sites: http//www.thecommonwealth.org
http//www.youngcommonwealth.org

Contents

	Page
Tables, Figures and Boxes	i
Acronyms and Abbreviations	iii
Currency Equivalents	v
Foreword	vi
Executive Summary	ix

Chapter 1: **Introduction**
1.1 Mauritian SMEs, Policies and the Asian Currency Crisis	1
1.2 Aim and Method	4
1.3 Concepts of Enterprise and National Competitiveness	5
1.4 Outline of the Study	7

Chapter 2: **Small Firms in International Markets**
2.1 Introduction	9
2.2 Past Export Achievements and the Current Climate	9
2.2.1 Historical Record	9
2.2.2 Structural Constraints	10
2.3 The SME and Micro-enterprise Population	12
2.3.1 The Magnitude of SMEs and Micro-enterprises	12
2.3.2 Industry-level Analysis of SMEs	16
2.4 Recent Trends in SME Manufactured Exports	18
2.4.1 EPZ SME Exports	19
2.4.2 Non-EPZ SME Exports	23
2.5 Conclusions	24

Chapter 3: **Evaluation of SME Capabilities**
3.1 Introduction	26
3.2 Competences	26
3.2.1 Marketing	26
3.2.1.1 Textiles	26
3.2.1.2 Printing and Publishing	29
3.2.1.3 IT	32
3.2.2 Design	34
3.2.2.1 Textiles	34
3.2.2.2 Printing and Publishing	35

3.2.3 Technology	36
3.2.3.1 Textiles	36
3.2.3.2 Printing and Publishing	38
3.2.3.3 IT	39
3.2.4 Human Resource Management	40
3.2.4.1 Investment in Training	40
3.2.4.2 Absenteeism and Staff Turnover	41
3.2.4.3 Wage Rates and Employee Education	42
3.2.4.4 Impressions of Organisational Culture	43
3.2.5 Conclusions	44
3.2.5.1 Marketing	45
3.2.5.2 Design	46
3.2.5.3 Technology	46
3.2.5.4 Human Resource	47
3.3 Strategy	48
3.3.1 Market Selection	48
3.3.2 Competitive Advantage	49
3.3.3 Conclusions	51
3.4 Managerial Characteristics	52
3.4.1 Commitment to Growth	52
3.4.2 Export Orientation	53
3.4.3 A Global or International Mindset	54
3.4.4 Conclusions	55

***Chapter 4*: Policy and Procedural Regime for SMEs**

4.1 Introduction	56
4.2 Policies and Procedures: SME Views	56
4.3 Selected Policy Impediments	59
4.3.1 Tariff Structure	59
4.3.2 Export Promotion	61
4.3.2.1 Access to Duty Free Imported Inputs	61
4.3.2.2 Overseas Marketing Support	62
4.3.3 Exchange Rate Management	64
4.3.4 Access to Finance	65
4.3.5 Other Policies to Foster Local Linkages and Clusters	70
4.4 Selected Procedural Impediments	72
4.4.1 The State of Procedural Obstacles	72
4.4.2 Small Business Start-up Problems	73
4.5 Infrastructure Impediments	77
4.6 Conclusions	78

Chapter 5: **The Institutional Support System for SMEs**
    5.1 Introduction   79
    5.2 Background on the SME Support System   79
    5.3 Enterprise Perceptions of SME Institutions   82
        5.3.1 SMIDO   82
        5.3.2 EPZDA   84
        5.3.3 MEDIA   86
        5.3.4 IVTB   88
        5.3.5 DBM   90
        5.3.6 Summary of Enterprise Perceptions   91
    5.4 Other Support Organisations   92
    5.5 An Assessment of the SME Support System   93
    5.6 Conclusions   94

Chapter 6: **Proposals to Promote SME Competitiveness**
    6.1 Introduction   95
    6.2 Macroeconomic Policies   95
    6.3 Trade Policies   96
        6.3.1 Import Liberalisation   96
        6.3.2 Export Promotion   96
    6.4 Bureaucratic Procedures   97
    6.5 Finance   98
    6.6 Technological Support   99
        6.6.1 Establish a Business Link   99
        6.6.2 Design House   100
        6.6.3 Textile Council   100
    6.7 Clusters and Linkages   100
    6.8 Human Capital   101
    6.9 Private Sector Initiatives   102
    6.10 Data Collection and Monitoring of SME Performance   103
    6.11 New Areas for SMEs   103

Appendix 1 – The Enterprise Survey   105
Appendix 2 – A Framework for Evaluating SME Capabilities   109
Appendix 3 – Permits and Clearances Required
        for the Setting Up of an Enterprise   113
Appendix 4 – Profiles of Selected Institutions and Policies for SMEs   115

Bibliography   125

Tables, Figures and Boxes

		Page
Tables		
2.1	Manufactured Export Performance in 1985-1996	10
2.2	Recent Growth of SMEs and Micro-enterprises in Manufacturing, 1992-1997	13
2.3	Employment Shares of SMEs in Manufacturing in Different Countries	15
2.4	Size Structure of Firms and Employment in the Manufacturing Sector, 1997	16
2.5	EPZ and Non-EPZ SMEs in the Manufacturing Sector in 1997	18
2.6	Manufactured Exports in SMEs and Large Firms in the EPZ, 1995-1997	20
2.7	Shares of SMEs and Large Firms in EPZ Exports, 1997	22
3.1	Use of Promotional Tools in the Textile Industry	27
3.2	Marketing Expenditure as a Percentage of Turnover in the Textile Industry	28
3.3	Use of Promotional Tools in the Printing and Publishing Industry	31
3.4	Marketing Expenditure as a Percentage of Turnover in the Printing and Publishing Industry	31
3.5	Products and Services Offered by Respondents in the IT Industry	32
3.6	Use of Promotional Tools in the IT Industry	33
3.7	Scoring System for Design	34
3.8	Investment in Training as a Percentage of Turnover	40
3.9	Significance of the Problem of Finding Appropriate Employee Skills	41
3.10	Average Monthly Wage in Mauritian Rupees	42
3.11	Summary of Competences	44
4.1	Tariffs on Finished Goods, July 1998	60
4.2	Commercial Bank Loans and Lending Rates to Small Scale Industries (SSI), 1995-1998	67
5.1	Overview of Institutions Supporting the SME Sector	80
5.2	User Perceptions of SMIDO Services	83
5.3	User Perceptions of EPZDA Services	86
5.4	User Perceptions of MEDIA Services	87
5.5	User Perceptions of IVTB Services	89

	5.6	User Perceptions of DBM Services	90
	5.7	Summary of User Perceptions of SME Support Services	91
	6.1	New Areas for SMEs in Textiles, Printing and IT	104
	A.1	Composition of Sample Survey	106

Figures

	2.1	Exports/employee in the EPZ, $41997	19
	2.2	Non-EPZ SME Exports, 1997 $m	23
	3.1	The Use of Designers in Sixteen Textile Companies	35
	3.2	The Use of Designers in Eight Printing and Publishing Companies	36
	3.3	Significance of Problem of Absenteeism	41
	4.1	Policy Obstacles to SMEs	59
	4.2	Trade-Weighted RER, 1994-98	65
	4.3	Time to Obtain All Permits to Start-Up	74
	4.4	Start-Up Permit Problems	76
	4.5	Infrastructure Problems	77
	A.1	Number of Companies Exporting and Their Destination	108
	A.2	Enterprise Dynamics and Exporting	110
	A.3	A Business Link for Mauritius	120

Boxes

	1.1	What is an SME?	8
	3.1	Bringing Printing to the High Street – The Case of Kall Kwik	46

Acronyms and Abbreviations

ASYCUDA	Automated System for Customs Data
CAD	Computer-aided design
CAE	Computer-aided engineering
CAM	Computer-aided manufacturing
CEO	Chief Executive Officer
CFTC	Commonwealth Fund for Technical Co-operation
CIB	Central Informatics Bureau
CPC	China Productivity Centre (Taiwan)
COMESA	Common Market for Eastern and Southern Africa
CPI	Consumer Price Index
CSO	Central Statistical Office (Mauritius)
DBM	Development Bank of Mauritius
EU	European Union
EDF	European Development Fund
EPZ	Export Processing Zone
EPZDA	Export Processing Zone Development Authority (Mauritius)
ERP	Effective Rate of Protection
FDI	Foreign Direct Investment
GDP	Gross Domestic Product
GATT	General Agreement on Trade and Tariffs
HKPC	Hong Kong Productivity Council
IDC	Industrial Development Committee (Mauritius)
IPA	Investment Promotion Agency
ISO	International Standards Organisation
IT	Information Technology
IVTB	Industrial and Vocational Training Board (Mauritius)
LE	Large Enterprise
MCA	Mauritius College of Art
ME	Micro Enterprise
MEDIA	Mauritius Export Development and Investment Authority
MEF	Mauritius Employer's Federation
MEPZA	Mauritius Export Processing Zone Authority
MFA	Multi Fibre Agreement
MGI	Mahatma Gandhi Institute (Mauritius)
MIE	Mauritius Institute of Education
MNC	Multi National Corporation
MOIC	Ministry of Industry and Commerce (Mauritius)

MPCC	Mauritius Productivity and Competitiveness Council
MSB	Mauritius Standard Bureau
MSTQ	Metrology, Standards, Testing and Quality
NAFTA	North American Free Trade Agreement
NCB	National Computer Board
NIC	New Industrial Countries
NIE	Newly Industrialising Economy
NIFT	National Institute of Fashion Technology
OECD	Organisation for Economic Cooperation and Development
PSDC	Penang Skills Development Centre (Malaysia)
PSE	Pioneer Status Enterprise
QC	Quality Control
R&D	Research and Development
RCA	Revealed Comparative Advantage
REER	Real Effective Exchange Rate
SADC	Southern African Development Community
SDR	Special Drawing Rights
SGS	Societe Generale de Surveillance
SIL	State Informatics Limited
SISIR	Singapore Institute of Standards and Industrial Research
SITC	Standard Industrial Trade Classification
SME	Small and Medium Enterprise
SMIDO	Small and Medium Industry Development Organisation (Mauritius)
SSEAM	Small Scale Entrepreneur Association of Mauritius
SUBEX-M	Subcontracting Exchange and Industrial Partnership Centre (Mauritius)
TC	Technological Capabilities
TDS	Technology Diffusion Scheme (Mauritius)
TQM	Total Quality Management
UN	United Nations
UNIDO	United Nations Industrial Development Organisation
UNDP	United Nations Development Programme
UoM	University of Mauritius
VAT	Value Added Tax
WTO	World Trade Organization
WWW	World Wide Web

Currency Equivalents

Rupees per US$ – Period averages	
1990	14.9
1991	15.7
1992	15.6
1993	17.7
1994	18.0
1995	17.4
1996	18.0
1997	20.6
1998	22.5

Source: IMF *International Financial Statistical Yearbook*, various

Foreword

Small businesses are the mainstay of the economies of most small states. Mauritius, a typical Commonwealth small island state with a population of just over 1 million, has a vibrant small business sector, with more than 5,700 small and medium enterprise (SMEs). This is a reflection of the market-friendly trade and investment policies Mauritius has pursued since the 1970s, as well as its skilled and literate workforce, relatively good infrastructure and pro-business government policy environment.

Recently the Government of Mauritius has looked increasingly to the small business sector to generate new exports and employment. Although some Mauritian SMEs have successfully broken into export markets, many others lacked the requisite technological and marketing capabilities to compete overseas. Moreover, the authorities had just begun some initiatives to encourage small firm exports and were actively seeking a new policy framework for SME export development.

In 1998, Mauritius approached the Commonwealth Secretariat for assistance for a strategy to boost the competitiveness of its SMEs. In response, a team from the Secretariat's Export and Industrial Development Division (EIDD) conducted this baseline study of SME exports and public policies in Mauritius. The study maps out the export record of Mauritian SMEs, assesses their technological and marketing capabilities, evaluates the progress of economic reform and deregulation policies, and examines the adequacy of services provided by SME support institutions. Drawing on best practice, the study also formulates a three-year strategy to increase SME exports from Mauritius. Among the key suggestions the report recommends are further import liberalisation, reductions in red tape (particularly business start-up regulations), setting up an export development fund for SMEs, commercialisation of the Development Bank of Mauritius, a re-organisation of SME institutions to create a Business Link, and business service delivery by SME associations. The Commonwealth Secretariat hopes to undertake similar baseline studies on small firms and public policies in other Commonwealth countries.

This study was undertaken for the Ministry of Industry and Commerce of Mauritius and executed with the assistance of the Small and Medium Industrial Development Organisation (SMIDO). It was financed by the Commonwealth Fund for Technical Co-operation, the Mauritian Ministry of Industry and Commerce and SMIDO. It is based on the findings of a Commonwealth mission to Mauritius between 20 July -7 August 1998 and subsequent desk research in London. The mission interviewed small firms, business organisations, consultancy firms, ministries and individuals. Following the mission, SMIDO helped with a postal questionnaire survey of SMEs in textiles, printing and information technology. Ganesh Wignaraja drafted chapters 1, 2 and 4 and Sue O'Neil 3 and 5. They jointly drafted chapter 6. The first draft of this report was discussed at a roundtable in Mauritius on 18 February 1999 involving the government, the private sector, labour organisations and the Commonwealth Secretariat. The comments of roundtable participants and the Ministry of Industry and Commerce were used to revise the report. On behalf of the Commonwealth Secretariat, I would like thank the Government of Mauritius, business associations and small firms for their support for this study.

R.N. Gold
Director
Export and Industrial Development Division

Executive Summary

1. Introduction

The island of Mauritius, because of its past industrial experience, has a large SME sector relative to its size of population. Our estimates suggest that there are about 25,761 SMEs and micro-enterprises (1997) in non-primary sector activities (of which 5,731 are in the manufacturing sector). SMEs and micro-enterprises account for 32.1% of total manufacturing employment, which is comparable to employment shares in advanced industrial countries (such as the UK, France and Korea) and well ahead of industrialising economies in Africa.

This study of the competitiveness of SMEs in the Mauritian manufacturing sector occurs at a time of the Asian currency crisis and great uncertainty in the international economy. The full impact of the Asian crisis upon Mauritian industry and its exports is not yet known. Before the onset of the crisis, it seemed that Mauritian industry would confront several economic threats in the early 21st Century: a severe deterioration in the international economic environment, falling world demand, volatile private capital flows, reduced foreign aid, rapid technological progress, and intense competition from low labour cost economies. The crisis will greatly add to these pressures as Asian firms restructure, become more efficient and globalise their production. The intense competition underlying this state of affairs suggests that to survive, more of Mauritian business has to match the productivity and technological capabilities of the best in the world.

The Government of Mauritius recognises this challenge and has developed a new export strategy, which was announced in the 1998 National Budget. This strategy emphasises new competitive advantages in manufacturing and services (e.g. high value added textiles, printing, offshore financial services, and information technology) and new policies and institutions for success. The 1998 Budget also mentions some useful initiatives for small firms (particularly, grants for technological upgrading) but a coherent approach to fostering SME competitiveness involving a mix of liberalisation and supply-side support has yet to be formulated. A dynamic, internationally competitive SME sector can contribute to economic growth, generate exports, foster diversification and increase employment. The addition of a coherent approach to SMEs competitiveness in the new export strategy would thus help to sustain future export dynamism in Mauritius.

This study assesses the export record of SMEs in Mauritius and provides suggestions on how to improve future SME competitiveness. The study represents a first attempt to synthesise what is known about the state of SME competitiveness during two weeks of fieldwork by a two-person Commonwealth team. It aims to do five things:

I. Examine the magnitude of the SME population in the manufacturing sector and its export performance, in overall terms and at an industry-level.

II. Use an enterprise survey, to highlight the marketing, technological, human capital and strategic strengths and weaknesses of SMEs in selected industrial and service sectors (e.g. textiles, printing and publishing and IT).

III. Analyse the influence of the outward-oriented, market-friendly policy regime on incentives for SME growth and competitiveness.

IV. Examine the role and adequacy of the support provided by public institutions for SME competitiveness.

V. Make suggestions for future SME competitiveness drawing on best practices in Commonwealth and non-Commonwealth economies.

At the request of SMIDO, the empirical part of this study defines SMEs as enterprises with 10-49 employees and micro-enterprises as those with less than 10 employees. Future work on small firms could usefully contemplate the application of of alternative definitions of firm size.

The study is based on a simple enterprise-level theory of comparative advantage. According to this theory, competitiveness arises at the level of individual firms with national competitiveness being the sum of the efficiency and dynamism of component firms in a given developing economy. The creation of enterprise (and hence national competitiveness) occurs through a risky and uncertain process of acquiring technological and other industrial capabilities in a system of imperfect factor markets (like finance, skills, information and technology). Government actions can enhance this process by removing economic distortions to enterprise growth and exporting as well as augmenting the workings of factor markets. This approach emphasises a combination of liberalisation/deregulation policies and structural policies (aimed at increasing education and training, technological activity and the supply of industrial finance) to enhance SME competitiveness. The private sector can also contribute to the design and implementation of national competitiveness strategies.

2. Small Firms in International Markets

As in other developing economies, time series information on the size structure of manufacturing activity and exports is difficult to ascertain in Mauritius. The study attempted to use available local data sources (from the Central Statistical Office and the Ministry of Industry and Commerce), supplemented by forecasting techniques, to develop a recent picture on the magnitude and competitiveness of small firms in the country. The most significant findings from our examination of the size and dynamism of the Mauritian SME sector are as follows:

- The industrial structure of the Mauritian manufacturing sector has a distinct dualistic pattern made up of many small firms and a few large firms. Our estimates suggest that of the 5,320 manufacturing establishments in 1997, 84.7% were micro-enterprises, 8.1% were SMEs and 7.2% were large firms. The relatively few large firms account for the bulk of manufacturing employment.

- After many years of expansion, it appears that the annual average growth rate of the number of large firms (-2.3%) and SMEs (-0.8%) has declined in 1992-1997 while the growth of micro-enterprises (4.3%) has increased. These trends should be viewed with caution because the figures for large firms and SMEs use actual data while those for micro-enterprises are unadjusted forecasts.

- In 1997, there were 467 SMEs, which collectively made a useful contribution to the Mauritian foreign exchange earnings by generating a total of $23.5 million worth of manufactured exports.

- However, as a group EPZ SMEs have been much more efficient in generating exports than non-EPZ SMEs. The value of manufactured exports from EPZ SMEs ($20.4 million) is over six times that of non-EPZ SMEs ($3.1 million) in 1997.

- EPZ SMEs (1.9%) made a negligible contribution to total EPZ exports in 1997 compared with large EPZ firms (98.1%). The aggregate figure masks the fact that SMEs seem to produce all the EPZ's flower exports and useful shares of EPZ exports of wood/paper products, other manufactured exports and watches and clocks.

- Total EPZ SME manufactured exports had a negative growth rate (-1.5% p.a.) in 1995-1997 compared with a low but positive growth rate for EPZ large firms (0.7%).

- The weak performance of EPZ SME exports is due to negative growth in several core activities (other manufactured products, food, flowers and textile yarn), the total decline of toys, and slow positive growth in wood/paper products. Three other items (jewellery, watches and clocks and electric and electronic products) had high positive growth. But, as these were from a small base, they had little influence on the overall export growth rate of SMEs.

- Interestingly, clothing (the single largest SME export) had respectable positive export growth.

- EPZ SMEs had lower ratios of exports per employee than large firms in most industrial branches in 1997. This simple and crude measure of labour productivity suggests that productivity in SMEs lags behind large firms in the EPZ.

- Survey estimates suggest that most non-EPZ SMEs produced entirely for the domestic market. Out of a total of 314 non-EPZ SMEs, about 26 only were engaged in exports in 1997. These firms exported very small shares of the country's exports of textiles, footwear and furniture.

- No data is available on the manufactured export performance of micro-enterprises but they were believed to be nearly all domestic market-oriented.

3. Evaluation of SME Capabilities

An enterprise survey was used to assess the export capabilities of SMEs in three industrial sectors (textiles, printing and publishing, and IT). This study broadly defines enterprise-level export capabilities in terms of: a) functional competences (i.e., the efficient use of marketing, design, technology and human resources); b) the ability to make informed strategic decisions about target markets and competitive positioning; and c) the managerial characteristics that influence export success (proxied by the commitment, orientation and attitude towards exporting of the head of the enterprise).

Marketing capabilities are evaluated in relation to the four principal elements of the marketing mix: product, price, promotion and distribution. In the textile industry, few SMEs appear to have a clear understanding of the concept of a target market or how branding can add value. These companies are making what they know how to make, rather than responding to customer demands. Consequently, most are producing far too broad a range of low quality, undifferentiated garments that are forced to compete heavily on price. The very small amount spent on promotion is channelled into expensive personal selling and virtually no use is made of more cost-effective promotional tools such as direct marketing. Few SMEs in the textile sector have developed ongoing arrangements with marketing intermediaries such as agents or distributors, and as such, business development initiatives tend to be largely reactive.

The less homogeneous sample of firms operating in the printing and publishing sector included jobbing printers (producing a broad range of relatively low quality, low-priced print mainly for the domestic market); specialist and higher quality printers (with a more clearly defined and value-added proposition targeting overseas markets or specific domestic market segments); and a number of companies operating in the pre-press or electronic media sector. At the lower end of this spectrum, price competition is fierce, little promotion is undertaken and only limited use is made of marketing intermediaries. At the higher end, established relationships with groups of target customers enables firms to deliver value at a profit.

The IT sector is even more diverse with firms engaged in selling computer hardware, software and consumables, as well as offering a variety of IT-based services. Once again, it is evident that companies which have a clearly defined proposition targeted at a distinct group of customers, with established channels to market, are best able to add value to their offer and maximise the effectiveness of their promotional spend. Overall, the IT sector appears to have better marketing strategies in place than the other two sectors.

The key to marketing competence is the development and implementation of a sound competitive marketing strategy, which in turn determines the nature, and specifies the tools, of the marketing mix. In the majority of instances, SMEs lack the necessary understanding of the role of, as well as the skills to develop, an effective marketing strategy. As such, their ability to compete in export markets is severely limited.

Design can add value to a company's proposition through its product (fashion design in textiles, and graphic design in printing and publishing), and through its branding and promotion (graphic design). The majority of SMEs in the textile and printing and publishing sectors are using some form of design resource. However, for design to be effective, it needs to be fully integrated into the strategy and processes of the company. Our observations suggest that design is under-utilised and that companies lack skills in setting design briefs and managing design projects.

In our sample, the majority of the SMEs in the textile industry use outdated production technologies. Investment in new plant and equipment is very low, little computerisation has been implemented in terms of CAD/CAM or sewing/stitching, processes tend to be still largely non-automated, and few management information or production control systems are in place. Quality control is mostly ad hoc and dependent on visual checking. Minimal use is made of technical consultants. Particular weaknesses are evident in production management and materials handling.

At the lower end of the printing and publishing sector, some machinery is so antiquated that it offers no chance at all of achieving any degree of export competitiveness. Here too, quality control is generally poor and the results of this are visually evident in print output. At the higher end, firms are using newer and more up-to-date machinery, and have in place better quality control systems. Across the board, technology for pre-press is good, or at least, adequate.

Unsurprisingly, technology in the IT sector is fit-for-purpose. Here, the major limitation is the cost and capability of the telecommunications infrastructure.

Of all the competences, human resources management seems weakest. A lack of HR skills is most apparent in the textile industry, marginally less so in printing and publishing, whilst the IT sector seems to be more progressive. However, it should be noted that, universally, the SME sector lags behind larger organisations in implementing state-of-the-art human resource management. Investment in training, as an indicator of management's commitment to its workforce, is very low across all three industry sectors. Absenteeism and staff turnover, as measures of employee commitment, are significant problems in the textile sector, moderate problems in printing and publishing, yet are substantially less problematic in IT. Similarly, as pointers to productivity, wage rates and levels of employee education are lowest in textiles and highest in IT. Organisational cultures tend to be more repressive in the textile industry, paternalistic in printing and publishing and more progressive in IT.

The table below summarises our assessment of SME competences.

Summary of competences

	Textiles
Marketing	
• Product	Product quality generally low Products lack differentiation Ranges too broad Limited use of branding
• Price	No use made of strategic pricing
• Promotion	Very low spend on promotion Overemphasis on peesonal selling Virtually no use made of direct marketing
• Distribution	Few arrangements with agents or distributors Underdevelopment of marketing channels
Design	Generally, design under-utilised Designers not integrated into business processes Lack of skills in setting design briefs and managing design projects
Technology	Outdated production technologies Weak in production management and materials handling Few management information systems Little use of technical consultants
Human resource	Investment in training low Major lack of employee skills Absenteeism a significant problem Staff turnover very high Low wage rates Low levels of employee education Culture sometimes repressive

Strategic capabilities are evaluated in terms of the ability to identify and select target markets, and to create and implement competitive advantage. The majority of firms in the sample lack skills in gathering market information and have no formal systems for ongoing market research. They make minimal use of the information services available. Additionally, there is very little evidence that SMEs can evaluate the potential of

Printing and publishing	IT
Jobbing printers: quality generally low; non-specialised Specialists: quality moderate to high Pre-press: high quality, clearly defined proposition	Products and services offered too diverse to comment on product or service range, quality, etc
Heavy price competition where value-add is low	No information on pricing
Low spend on promotion Limited use of the total range of promotional tools	More varied use of promotional tools, particularly electronic media
Limited use of marketing intermediaries	More varied use of marketing channels
Limited use of design resource	
Antiquated machinery, particularly in the smaller companies Quality control generally poor Pre-press capabilities adequate Little use of technical consultants	Level of technology consistent with business objectives
Investment in training low Major lack of employee skills Absenteeism a moderate problem Staff turnover moderate Moderate wage rates Low levels of employee education	Investment in training very low Major lack of employee skills Absenteeism manageable Staff turnover is not a problem Attractive wage rates Moderate levels of education

future or current markets or can assess the strategic fit between their own capabilities and the requirements of the market. In particular, it is doubtful that most SMEs have sufficient understanding of cost or management accounting to evaluate the potential financial returns of specific strategic choices.

The principal sources of competitive advantage for SMEs are widely cited as the development of a niche strategy, offering meaningful and differentiated propositions to a limited number of markets, and developing good relations with overseas distributors and agents. SMEs, particularly in the textile sector but also in printing and publishing, generally fail to tap into these sources of advantage. Nor do they utilise new digital technologies, which can help the small business sector in developed economies to overcome its inherent disadvantages of size, scale and location in order to compete effectively in the global market.

As with the marketing strategy, the SME sector lacks the ability to develop effective corporate strategies. There is little evidence of high-quality strategic thinking or forward business planning. Few companies appear to prepare a three- or five-year business plan, the principle framework for formulating strategy. Without this strategic perspective, SMEs are poorly placed to develop export competitiveness.

Increasingly, debate on SME competitiveness focuses on managerial characteristics, specifically the commitment of the owner-manager to growth and exporting; the export orientation of the owner-manager in terms of perception of risk and willingness to commit resources; and the personal mindset of the owner-manager in terms of his/her global perspective. The survey of SMEs indicates weak managerial skills in owner-managers. This is because the owner-manager resists relinquishing maximum control and/or owing to lack of resources, professional management from outside is never implemented. As a result growth is limited and export opportunities are missed. It is clear from the sample that where owner-managers rate exporting as a priority and are willing to take risk and commit resources, the company becomes a more successful exporter. However, most SMEs see exporting as "nice to have", rather than their principal strategic thrust. An additional factor that is apparent in the survey is that owner-managers who have a global or international mindset, usually developed during long periods of abroad, are significantly more able to develop and capitalise on export potential. Those who are limited in their personal horizons have more difficulty in adopting an export orientation.

4. Policy and Procedural Regime for SMEs

The influence of the trade, industrial and macroeconomic regime on SME competitiveness has been assessed using macroeconomic data and the enterprise survey. The overall conclusion is that the present policy environment is more favourable to small firms than it has been previously due to two decades of gradual liberalisation and deregulation of government controls. The country is fortunate to have escaped a strong or pronged inward-orientation, which hampered many developing countries since the 1960s and 1970s. The Mauritian policy environment is more open and small business-friendly than those of many competitors in Africa and the Indian Sub-Continent. Economic policy is generally well managed and more predictable than most. The private sector is also consulted before major policy initiatives are implemented and their views often shape policy.

Major areas of policy success include switching from quantitative restrictions to tariffs (and cuts in tariffs), the lack of public procurement and local content rules, maintaining a depreciated real exchange rate, removal of exchange controls, maintaining a liberal and market-oriented banking system, the introduction of VAT, and streamlining some administrative procedures. This is an impressive record and makes Mauritian enterprises more poised than others to reap future gains from globalisation of trade and investment.

Inspite of past successes in policy reform, however, there is still room for improvement, which could benefit small firms as well as the rest of the Mauritian private sector.

- Although the average tariff for manufacturing is about 30% (1994), tariff reform is far from complete and the existing protective structure discriminates against small firms particularly those in the non-EPZ sector. Some sectors with a large population of SMEs (including food products, footwear and furniture) are very highly protected while the remainder receives negligible protection. The economic rationale for this protective structure and the future agenda on tariff reform are unclear.

- Small firms lack ready access to duty-free imported inputs to offset an anti-export bias in the trade regime. This seems to be linked to processing delays in the instruments to access such inputs and the lack of coherent guidelines for raw material wastage provision.

- Until fairly recently, there was little effective overseas marketing support for small firms. MEDIA has improved service delivery in this regard (and is working with SMIDO to identify SME exporters) but the take-up rate among small firms has been quite low. This raises questions about the quantity and quality of the services provided.

- There are several problems connected with the supply of industrial finance for SMEs. Small firms face higher real interest rates (ranging between 11-20%), more restrictive terms for bank loans, and less access to commercial bank finance than large firms. These problems are classic symptoms of imperfections in capital markets, which give rise to a "large firm bias" in the allocation of bank finance.

- There is an absence of effective policies to develop linkages and industrial clusters among small firms. SUBEX-M – the only scheme which provides information about potential intra-firm production linkages – started very recently but has run into trouble following the phasing out of technical assistance from an international donor. It is also focussed on high skill engineering industries in which Mauritius has no obvious short or medium-term comparative advantage viz-a-vis world markets. Low skill industries in which the country has an existing/medium-term comparative advantage (such as textiles and clothing, leather products and footwear, and food products) are excluded.

- Serious administrative barriers to small firm start-up raise transactions costs to SMEs above those of competitor economies. The sample shows a wide variation in bureaucratic processing times for small firm start-up – in the best case, all start-up procedures can be completed in 0-3 months but the worst can be in excess of 10 months. The worst case results are a particular concern. Long processing delays arise from a multi-stage approval process involving enterprise contact with 11 different public agencies. Start-up procedures have raised operating costs above optimum levels, wasted scarce management time, employment of additional staff to deal with redundant paperwork, acted as an obstacle to efforts to adopt quick response practices, and provided incentives for rent-seeking behaviour by public officials.

- On the whole, Mauritian SMEs do not seem to view infrastructural impediments as a major obstacle to exporting. Some aspects of infrastructure are considered quite efficient by small firms (e.g. water supply and sewage, airport facilities and telecommunications reliability). The cost and availability of air freight are a problem to small and large firms alike. This is closely followed by weaknesses in electricity supply (both voltage fluctuations and breakdowns). Customs clearance is also regarded as a problem by some small firms.

5. The Institutional Support System for SMEs

The institutional support system for SMEs is examined from two perspectives: (a) how effective is it as a complete framework to meet the needs of SMEs and help them to improve their competitiveness? (b) how do SMEs themselves perceive the adequacy of service delivery by SME institutions?

For the size of the country and its stage of development, Mauritius has a particularly wide range of support services for the SME sector. The system of business development services involves several agencies mostly under the umbrella of the Ministry of Industry and Commerce. These include: SMIDO, directly mandated with providing support to small and medium manufacturing enterprises; EPZDA, concerned with supporting firms in the Export Processing Zone; MEDIA, whose triple roles involve export promotion, attracting FDI and the management of industrial estates; IVTB, providing educational or training courses geared predominantly to the SME sector; and DBM, offering finance to SMEs at preferential rates. In addition, other public-sector organisations, such as MSB, TDS, SUBEX-M and NCB, provide services that SMEs can draw on. The private sector also contains some trade and industry associations but only one, SSEAM, is directly concerned with supporting SMEs.

The institutional support system for SME as a whole has many strengths. SMEs are offered a very wide choice of support (including training, consultancy, market research, help with start-up, technical and information services, preferential access to trade fairs, contact promotion programmes, and financial assistance in the form of both loans and grants). In addition, individual SME institutions demonstrate a high degree of motivation, enthusiasm and commitment to the development of the SME sector.

However, the export performance of SMEs, as detailed in Chapter 2, indicates that the investment in SME support is not delivering the growth required or expected at the enterprise level. This failure in the effectiveness of the institutional support system is partly due to a lack of co-ordination and coherence within the diversity of supporting organisations. The historical emergence of individual entities, without a clear guiding vision for the complete framework, has created gaps in support and duplication of service offers.

In particular, we suggest that the following issues need the most urgent attention. If improved, these areas could deliver the most significant benefits:

- Developing a strategic perspective of the SME sector as a whole and its role within the spectrum of Mauritian commercial activity.
- Enhancing co-ordination between the different institutions so as to ensure comprehensiveness whilst avoiding duplication.
- Incorporating more commercial accountability in order to improve and monitor effectiveness.
- Targeting SMEs on an industry basis in order to more closely tailor services to needs.
- Adopting a more proactive stance in directing SMEs to the help they need, rather than allowing them simply to choose from a menu of options.
- Exploiting more innovative approaches to SME support.
- Enhancing the levels of managerial skill and expertise within individual institutions.
- Developing and utilising the potential of the private sector in supporting SMEs.

The survey results on small enterprise perceptions of SME institutions were interesting. There is evidence of a respectable level of awareness of the services offered by individual institutions (between 65% to 73% of the sample SMEs have heard of given services provided by different institutions). In contrast, usage of the services is low (only between 14% to 23% of the sample SMEs have actually used given services provided by different institutions). Those small firms that do take advantage of the services on offer evaluated their usefulness (on a scale of 1 to 5, where 5 is the most useful) and find such services to vary in usefulness (between 3.8 to 4.7 depending on the service).

Given the small size of Mauritius and the intensity of support, the level of awareness suggests some room for improvement. This is also true of users' perceptions of usefulness. However, the extremely low level of take-up should concern all the institutions and the reasons for this should be more closely examined. These findings also suggest that the SME support system, as a total entity, should be redesigned in order to deliver enhanced benefits.

6. Proposals to Promote SME Competitiveness

Drawing on Chapters 1-5, the mission was been able to develop a menu of proposals to promote SME competitiveness in Mauritius. In the light of the analytical framework discussed above, the report adopts a market-friendly approach to SME competitiveness as distinct from a bureaucratic-led strategy. It adopts a holistic approach emphasising the removal of economic distortions and the correction of market imperfections in skills, technology and finance. It also accords strong roles for both the government and the private sector in implementation of the proposals and recognises that a staged approach is conducive to success.

It is hoped that the proposals would achieve the following objectives:

(a) removal of policy and institutional impediments to direct SME exporting;

(b) reduction of policy and institutional obstacles to indirect exporting from SMEs (i.e., sub-contracting/supplier relations between SMEs and large export firms).

These proposals cover several areas: macroeconomic management, trade policy, bureaucratic procedures, finance, technological support, clusters and linkages, human capital, private sector initiatives and data collection and monitoring of SME's performance. The attached table contains the detailed suggestions arranged by strategic thrust, implementing agency and time frame. Further work needs to be done to refine and translate these proposals into concrete actions.

SME Competitiveness Strategy for Mauritius: Strategic Thrust, Actions and Time Frame

ISSUES	STRATEGIC THRUST	POSSIBLE IMPLEMENTING AGENCY
Macroeconimic Management	Maintain a stable, macroeconomic climate to induce SME and private investment	Ministry of Finance, Bank of Mauritius
Trade Policy	Achieve a low, uniform effective rate of protection of 15% within 4 years to encourage SME upgrading	Ministry of Finance with an international economic consultancy firm
	Provide duty-free access to imported inputs to all SMEs exporters	Ministry of Finance
	Offset anti-export bias of trade regime for SMEs via export promotion	MEDIA with Business Associations
Bureaucratic Procedures	Streamline procedures for new firm start-up	Ministry of Industry and Commerce, SMIDO
	Streamline approval procedures for FDI and joint ventures with SMEs	Ministry of Finance/Ministry of Industry and Commerce
	Investigate all residual procedures affecting SMEs	Ministry of Industry and Commerce with Business Associations and SMDIO
Finance	Improve access to finance for SME	Ministry of Finance MEDIA, DBM, SME Associations
	Reduce real interest rates for SME lending	
Technological Support	Provide co-ordinated support framework for SMEs	Ministry of Industry and Commerce, SMIDO
	Enhance design skills in SMEs	Mauritius Productivity and Competitiveness Council, EPZDA
	Create a dedicated support institution for the textile sector	Ministry of Industry and Commerce, EPZDA

SHORT-TERM 1999	MEDIUM-TERM 2000-2002
• Develop a plan to reduce the budget deficit by 25% within 3 years. • Persist with a competitive real exchange rate • Restore low, stable real interest rates	• Implement budget deficit plan through civil service and public enterprise reform • Maintain competitive real exchange and interest rates
• Re-activate programme of import liberalisation. • Create a tariff reform committee to manage the import reforms	• Implement tariff reforms and monitor results
• Streamline EPZ certificate and duty drawback schemes. • Develop raw material wastage provision for all potential exports	• Continue to achieve greater efficiency in processing times and update wastage provisions
• Consolidate export promotion activities into a major event "Mauritius Week" • Establish a dedicated web site for SME exporters	• Create Trade Promotion Offices in key markets (USA, Europe and Africa) as joint ventures between government and business associations • Establish a network of shops for tourists as joint ventures between government and business associations
• Reform local government permits • Reform work/residence permits	• Monitor processing times for new firm start-up
• Implement the Board of Investment	• Monitor processing times for BOI approvals
• Commission a comprehensive "red tape analysis" for all procedures affecting SMEs	• Implement the results of the red tape analysis • Set clear, uniform guidelines for all SME procedures and monitor standards.
• Create an Export Development Fund for SMEs from privatisation of MEDIA/DBM industrial estates • Foster Credit Unions in SME associations	• Commercialise the DBM • Implement the Venture Capital Fund;
• Implement the Mutual Guarantee Fund	• Publicise and support Mutual Guarantee Fund
• Undertake feasibility study for a Business Link for SMEs along UK lines	• Establish Business Link by subsuming SMIDO and other relevant business services
• Actively seek out top designers for short-term consultancies	• Undertake a feasibility study for a Design House and implement results
• Undertake a feasibility study for transforming EPZDA into a textile council	• Implement results of feasibility study

SME Competitiveness Strategy for Mauritius: Strategic Thrust, Actions and Time Frame *continued*

ISSUES	STRATEGIC THRUST	POSSIBLE IMPLEMENTING AGENCY
Clusters & Linkages	Promote industrial clusters for textiles and clothing and food products	Ministry of Industry and Commerce, SMIDO
	Foster development of clusters and networks	Mauritius Competitiveness and Productivity Council
Human Capital	Reduce skill gaps in potential areas of comparative advantage	Ministry of Education; Ministry of Industry and Commerce; Business Associations
	Increase certification and tailor made skills for industry	IVTB
	Reduce Absenteeism rates in industry	Ministry of Industry and Commerce
Private Sector Initiatives	Strengthen SME associations	Small firms with support from government
	Actively seek SME members in existing business associations	Existing business associations
	Actively support service delivery by Business Link	Business associations, consultancy firms, enterprises
	Deepen commercial banks links with SMEs	Commercial banks
	Reduce skill gaps in potential areas of comparative advantage	Business associations and enterprises
Data Collection & Monitoring of SMEs Performance	Develop a consistent definition of SMEs	Ministry of Industry & Commerce, SMIDO
	Create a database on SME performance	CSO, SMIDO

SHORT-TERM 1999	MEDIUM-TERM 2000-2002
• Absorb SUBEX within SMIDO • Remove procedural obstacles to indirect exporting	• Develop and implement a programme to upgrade suppliers
• Commission research by consultancy firms on industry/market-specific opportunities	• Attract FDI and large firm into clusters • Implement results of research
• Develop more sandwich courses at university for gaining industrial skills • Introduce a programme to attract back Mauritian professionals from overseas	• Provide more scholarships for overseas studies in relevant skills
• Re-focus on core business of designing and delivering academically validated vocational education and training courses	• Pass involvement in short-courses to the private sector • IVTB should monitor quality of private sector training
• Introduce a "Don't Miss Monday Campaign"	• Monitor results of "Don't Miss Monday Campaign" and repeat if necessary
• Re-position Small Scale Entrepreneur Association of Mauritius as a federation of individual SME associations • New Federation to advocate SME case & deliver services • Set up an information/resource centre for SMEs • Publicise services & benefits of membership • Develop SME services • JEC membership for SME associations	• Establish industrial associations for key SME sectors
• Provide consultants • Advise on industrial problems & future services	• Provide feedback on services • Develop export houses and export consultancies
• Appoint specialist small business advisors • Undertake staff training to better understand SME needs	• Undertake relevant research on SMEs • Feedback sector-specific information to government & SME Federation
• Provide more short in-plant placements for university students	• Launch training centres/schemes for training of middle management, production management and design skills
• Universal adoption of new definition of SMEs	• Consistently apply definition of SMEs
• Develop key SME performance indicators • Develop an annual survey of SME perceptions of the policy environment & institutions	• Continue with annual survey of SME performance and perceptions • Use SME survey to inform future policy making

1 Introduction

1.1 Mauritian SMEs, Policies and the Asian Currency Crisis

Mauritius, because of its past industrial experience, has a large small and medium enterprise (SME) sector relative to its population size. Our estimates suggest that there are about 25,761 SMEs and micro-enterprises (1997) in non-primary sector activities (see Chapter 2). 5,731 of these are in the manufacturing sector. SMEs and micro-enterprises account for 32.1% of total manufacturing employment. This figure is comparable to employment shares in advanced industrial countries (such as the UK, France and Korea) and well ahead of industrialising economies in Africa. While the size of the SME/micro-enterprise sector is documented in Mauritian publications, little is known about its record of competitiveness on international markets and its future prospects.

This study of the competitiveness of SMEs in the Mauritian manufacturing sector has been conducted at a time of crisis and uncertainty in the international economy. Since the second half of 1997, the East and South-East Asia has been engulfed in a financial crisis which has lasted more than a year. The sharp reversals for some of the world's fastest growing economies and the greater caution of international investors have chilled world economic growth.[1] Economic theory suggests that most of initial impact of the crisis will be felt inside Asia itself and it will take some time to spread elsewhere. Two kinds of transmission mechanism are associated with the contagion from Asia:

- Whether an economy outside Asia will be affected by primary effects of the crisis will depend on the degree to which it has developed trade and investment (as well as tourism, aid and capital market) linkages with the East and South-East Asian economies.

- A given economy may suffer secondary effects arising from the impact of the crisis on the US and EU economies.

To what extent is Mauritius likely to be affected by the contagion?

Take the primary effects of the crisis. There are no aid linkages with Asia and little inflow of tourism from Asia. Mauritius is also relatively insulated from an external shock in its direct trading linkages with East and South-East Asia — for instance, East Asian economies (largely Singapore and Hong Kong) accounted for less than 1% of EPZ exports

---

[1] For the best and most up to date work on the Asian crisis see the IMF World Economic Outlook., published twice a year.

in 1996 while the EU (71.3%) and the US (18%) accounted for the bulk of these exports.[2] However, Mauritius is less insulated from a shock from its direct investment linkages with Asia. Hong Kong and China alone made-up about one third of Actual FDI inflows in 1990-1997 while the EU economies account for the most of the remainder.[3]

Secondary effects are likely to be even more significant than direct shocks because the EU and the US economies are Mauritius's major trading partners and the EU is its major source of inward investment. Consequently, manufactured exports from Mauritius may decline as the Asian crisis causes slower growth in the EU and US economies and as competition increases from Asian economies that have devalued their currencies. The latest OECD forecasts for world GDP growth are quite pessimistic -the 1999 GDP forecast for the 29 leading economies was recently cut from 2.5% to 1.9%[4]. Similarly, between July 1997 and February 1998, alone the currencies of the South and South-East Asian economies have depreciated between 50% and 231% against the US$.[5] At the time of writing, world growth still appears unstable in the short-term and tit-for-tat devaluations have intensified.

The full impact of the Asian crisis upon Mauritian industry and its manufactured exports is not yet known. Before the onset of the crisis, it seemed that Mauritian industry would confront several related economic threats in the early 21st Century: a severe deterioration in the international economic environment, falling world demand, volatile private capital flows, reduced foreign aid, rapid technological progress, and intense competition from low labour cost economies. The Asian crisis will greatly add to these pressures as Asian firms' restructure, become more efficient and globalise their production.

The intense competition underlying this scenario suggests one thing: to survive, more of Mauritian business has to match the productivity and technological capabilities of the best in the world. The Government of Mauritius also needs to support enterprise competitiveness with a coherent strategy for industrial adjustment. Mauritius can be viewed as a pioneer in the Commonwealth for its new export strategy, which was announced in the 1998 Budget of the Minister of Finance.[6] This strategy emphasises the growth of products that already have a competitiveness advantage in world markets and the development of new competitive advantages in manufacturing and services. The government has also institutionalised the process of strategic export thinking in a newly created Mauritius Productivity and Competitiveness Council. These initiatives will give Mauritian business a "first mover advantage" over neighbouring African economies and some South Asian economies.

A hitherto somewhat neglected aspect of industrial policy adjustment in Mauritius is the potential contribution that can be made by SMEs. Policy attention was

---

[2] Bank of Mauritius (1997), p. 106.
[3] Estimated from FDI data provided by the Bank of Mauritius.
[4] The OECD forecast was reported in The Guardian 16 November 1998, p. 26.
[5] UN World Investment Report 1998, p. 210. The currency deprecations are: Indonesia (231%), Korea (83%), Malaysia (55.4%), Philippines (51.4%) and Thailand (87.1%).
[6] The Commonwealth Secretariat provided technical assistance in developing the new export strategy and advised the Government in the 1998 pre-budget consultations with the private sector. The assistance was based on Lall and Wignaraja (1998).

traditionally geared to encouraging the entry of foreign direct investment and the growth of large firms. It was implicitly assumed that SME growth and exporting automatically follow suit. In this regard too, the 1998 National Budget saw the beginning of a more active approach to SME promotion. For the first time in the country's history, a specific package of measures was announced for SME development:

1. A National Entrepreneurs Bank promoted by the Development Bank of Mauritius (DBM) and the State Investment Corporation of Mauritius.
2. Five new industrial estates for SMEs run by the Mauritius Export Development and Investment Authority (MEDIA).
3. Feasibility study grants from the Small and Medium Industry Development Organisation (SMIDO) on a cost-sharing basis to potential SMEs.
4. Product and process development grants from SMIDO which covers up to 50% of direct project cost of new products and processes.
5. Training grants for technical and managerial education of employees of SMEs.
6. Some land in the Freeport Zone to assist SMEs in the marketing of their products.

Recent budgetary policy is influenced by a more pro-SME emphasis in industrial policy by the Ministry of Industry and Commerce (MOIC). A fundamental element of MOIC's approach is to enhance the competitiveness of small firms in Mauritius. The MOIC has attempted to foster a collective approach to small firm service delivery by SMIDO and MEDIA and to source technical assistance. In this vein, in 1999, the MOIC received a European Union grant of about 6 million ECUs to provide 50:50 cost-sharing grants for consultancy services to upgrade products and processes; to establish a Mutual Guarantee Fund and Equity Participation Fund for easier access to finance; and to provide training for management and export development.[7] It also obtained assistance from the Commonwealth Fund for Technical Co-operation (CFTC) to undertake this diagnostic study of small firm exports, policies and support institutions.

The move towards a small firm focus in budgetary/industrial policy is a welcome development for the country. Moreover, some of the actions mentioned above are useful interventions for small firms. However, a coherent approach to foster competitiveness in SMEs of the type witnessed in successful SME-driven economies (such as the UK, Ireland, Singapore and Taiwan) still appears to be absent in Mauritius. These economies are able to sequence economic liberalisation with a comprehensive package of support services to SMEs involving finance, technology, training and marketing. The two together provide a "push and pull" effect for small firms to upgrade and become competitive. There is also a general dearth of policy analysis and data on

---

[7] Further details of this project are contained in MOIC (1997).

SME issues in Mauritius, which confirms our impression that historically the subject was not in the forefront of economic policy.[8] The Government of Mauritius is aware of these gaps and is searching for solutions to remedy them.

Changes in the nature of business world-wide are tending to favour the resurgence of the SME sector as a global player.[9] Consumer preferences are moving towards specialised and customised products, creating niche markets that are more easily met by small-scale flexible and adaptable enterprise structures. Paradoxically the globalisation of business creates the need for localised supply chains, comprising numerous small businesses subcontracting to larger ones, in order to deliver faster and more efficiently. Developments in communications technologies are minimising the requirements for physical presence, facilitating the "downsizing" of the large, monolithic company and the emergence of the virtual organisation, and thus revitalising the role that SMEs can play in the world economy. A dynamic internationally competitive SME sector would also contribute to economic growth, generate exports, alleviate foreign exchange constraints, increase employment opportunities and reduce poverty. These trends reinforce the need to add another leg to the new export strategy in Mauritius by fully integrating the role of SMEs in the bid for greater enterprise and hence national competitiveness.

1.2 Aim and Method

The objective of this study is to assess the export competitiveness record of SMEs in Mauritius and to suggest policy improvements for future SME performance. To this end, the study aimed to:

1. Examine the magnitude of the SME population in the manufacturing sector and its export performance, in overall terms and at an industry-level.

2. Use an enterprise survey, to highlight the marketing, technological, human capital and strategic strengths and weaknesses of SMEs in selected industrial and service sectors.

3. Analyse the influence of the outward-oriented, market-friendly policy regime on incentives for SME growth and competitiveness.

4. Examine the role and adequacy of the support provided by public institutions for SME competitiveness.

5. Make suggestions for future SME competitiveness drawing on best practices in Commonwealth and non-Commonwealth economies.

It is a first attempt to synthesise what is known about the state of SME development in the country, the nature of manufacturing capabilities of small firms, the policy and

---

[8] The few available papers and studies on SMEs include: SMIDO (1996), Jeetun (1997), and De Chazel du Mee (1998).
[9] See Humprey and Schmitz (1996), DTI (1996) and UN, World Investment Report 1998.

institutional obstacles facing small firms, the quality of business services provided to small firms by public sector institutions, and what might be done to help small firms grow and compete overseas. The study does not claim to be comprehensive in its coverage of firms, sectors, policies and institutions. The two-person Commonwealth team did what it could in about two weeks of fieldwork and some months of data processing and report writing. More work needs to be done by Mauritian institutions to refine and implement the findings of this study.

1.3 Concepts of Enterprise and National Competitiveness

The framework for this study is based on an enterprise-level theory of comparative advantage. Studies by economic historians from Joseph Schumpeter onwards suggest that technological change is the principal source of industrial growth and rising living standards in both developed and developing economies. In general, developing countries lag well behind developed countries in their technological and other industrial capabilities because of differences in scientific and engineering manpower, R&D infrastructure, industrial experience and expenditure on R&D. Within developing countries too, there are large technology and productivity gaps between best practice and other firms. Building on this work, new theoretical approaches in economics suggest that competitiveness arises at the level of the manufacturing enterprise with national competitiveness being the sum of the efficiency and dynamism of component firms within a given developing economy.[10] The creation of enterprise (and hence national competitiveness) occurs through a risky and uncertain process of acquiring technological and other industrial capabilities in a system of imperfect factor markets (like finance, skills, information and technology).

Many external factors – such as initial economic conditions, the international economic environment, luck and policy support (to remedy market imperfections) – influence the learning process at enterprise-level. Of these, policy support is probably the most important determinant of success (and is the only one that can be readily influenced). Commonwealth experience suggests that most developing countries can reap the rewards of liberalisation and structural adjustment programmes compared with inward-oriented, state dominated development strategies. In order to capitalise on these gains, markets and governments need to work together to evolve coherent national competitiveness strategies, which promote policies to reduce domestic distortions in markets and those to accelerate technological change in enterprises. Successful national competitiveness strategies feature the following elements:

- A stable, predictable macroeconomic environment for enterprise development characterised by low budget deficits, tight inflation control and competitive real exchange rates.

[10] See Lall and Wignaraja (1998), Wignaraja (1998 and 1999) for elaboration of this approach to comparative advantage.

- An outward-oriented, market-friendly trade and industrial regime emphasising dismantling of import controls and tariffs. This signals industry to restructure and develop a strong export push (duty-free access to raw materials and assistance for export marketing).

- A pro-active foreign investment strategy which emphasises targeting of a few realistic sectors and host countries, overseas promotion offices as public-private partnerships, competitive investment incentives and radically streaming investment approval processes.

- Sustained investments in human capital at all levels (particularly tertiary-level scientific, information technology and engineering education) and increased enterprise training (with assistance for industry associations to launch training schemes, accompanied by an information campaign to educate firms about the benefits of training and tax breaks for training).

- Comprehensive technology support for quality management, productivity improvement, metrology and technical services for small and medium enterprises (including grants for SMEs to obtain ISO9000 certification, creating productivity centres and commercialisation of public technology institutions).

- Access to sufficient industrial finance at competitive interest rates through prudent monetary policy management, competition in the banking sector, training for bank staff in assessing SME lending risks and specialist soft loans for SMEs.

- An efficient and cost-competitive infrastructure with respect to air and sea cargo, telecommunications, Internet access and electricity. This might include liberalisation of air and sea cargo entry and commercialisation/privatisation of infrastructure parastatals with effective regulation.

Some of these elements, for instance macroeconomic management and outward-orientation, are a part of standard structural adjustment programmes. Others (such as human development, technology support and targeted foreign investment promotion) go furhter but are still consistent with a market-friendly approach to industrial export development.

In a market economy, the main role for the private sector is to become productive and generate national wealth. Business associates assist industry by advocating the case for business and deregulation. With a rising share of private sector activity in GDP, however, the private sector needs to move beyond its traditional function of wealth creation and advocating the case for business. The private sector itself can make an important contribution in designing and implementing national competitiveness strategies in developing countries. This pro-active role can include: helping government to plug information gaps through participation in national policy making bodies and international trade negotiations; augmenting government capabilities via short-term secondment programmes of private sector managers and technicians; participating in infrastructure projects through joint finance and management skills; and helping weaker firms to help themselves via creating industry-specific training centres and other actions.

In formulating coherent competitiveness strategies, governments and markets should bear in mind that a number of negative factors could hinder successful outcomes. These impediments include: weak government capabilities to design and implement competitiveness strategies; a lack of government commitment to reform; poor relations between the government and the private sector; deteriorating macroeconomic conditions; and political instability. Experience indicates that countries that take steps to mitigate or reduce the impact of these impediments are more likely to succeed than others.

1.4 Outline of the Study

The study is set out as follows.

Chapter 2 examines the magnitude of the SME and micro-enterprise population in the manufacturing sector and its recent manufactured export performance. It looks at the export propensities of EPZ and non-EPZ SMEs, the export performance of EPZ SMEs compared to large EPZ firms at an industry-level (export growth, productivity and export shares by skill intensity) and the pattern of exports from non-EPZ SMEs. The lack of data on these issues confines this analysis to either the post-1992 period or post-1995 period. Longer time series analysis would be valuable to investigate whether the short/medium-run trends in SME exporting behaviour hold over the long-term.

Chapter 3 examines the capabilities of a sample of Mauritian SMEs in three critical industries (textiles, printing and publishing, and information technology). It looks at marketing, design, technology, human capital competences as well as strategic capabilities.

Chapter 4 analyses the nature of key macroeconomic, trade and industrial policies in Mauritius particularly as they affect the fostering of competitiveness of SMEs. The coverage includes import liberalisation, export promotion, exchange rates, industrial finance, bureaucratic procedures, policies for clusters and linkages, and infrastructure.

Chapter 5 analyses the nature, coverage, adequacy and service delivery of the key public sector SME institutions. The focus is on those institutions dealing with marketing, human capital and technological needs of small firms. Private sector SME institutions were excluded from the analysis.

Chapter 6 draws on the findings of the previous chapters to present policy suggestions for enhancing the competitiveness of small firms in international markets.
The four appendices present the SME survey, the framework used for evaluating SME capabilities, a list of the permits and clearances required for the setting up of an enterprise in Mauritius (including an SME), and suggestions for new institutions and policies. There is also a detailed bibliography.

At the request of SMIDO, the empirical part of this study defines SMEs as enterprises with 10-49 employees and micro-enterprises as those with less than 10 employees. When SMEs and micro-enterprises are mentioned together, this means all firms with less than 50 employees. Future work on small firms could usefully consider the use of alternative definitions of firm size (see Box 1.1).

Box 1.1:   What is an SME?

Several different criteria can be used to distinguish between SMEs and large firms in an economy. The three most popular benchmarks are: the value of production equipment, the value of sales and the number of employees. Each of these has its relative merits. However, setting the cut-off point between an SME and a large firm is more difficult and can vary depending on the level of development, the structure of an economy, and the characteristics of particular production technologies. Under its 1993 Industrial Expansion Act, Mauritius defines an SME as one whose production equipment does not exceed 10 million Mauritian Rupees. Unfortunately, this definition cannot be used in our empirical work as national data collection agencies (such as the Central Statistical Office of Mauritius) rely on employment rather than production equipment to capture firm size. Apart from this practical issue, an employment-based definition is more appropriate to distinguish between manufacturing and services activities. As skills (rather than equipment) drive services, production equipment would be a misleading indicator of firm size in this regard. These considerations suggest the need for a new definition for SMEs in Mauritius. For simplicity, an SME in manufacturing could be a firm with less than 50 employees and in services one with less than 20 employees. In both cases, they should be firms that are independent and not a subsidiary of a larger organisation.

2 Small Firms in International Markets

2.1 Introduction

This chapter examines the recent export performance of SMEs in the manufacturing sector in Mauritius as a background to the study. It examines the following: (a) past achievements and the current climate for manufactured exports; (b) the magnitude of the SME and micro-enterprise population in manufacturing; and (c) the manufactured export performance of SMEs in the EPZ and non-EPZ sectors (where possible relative to large firms). This study defines SMEs as enterprises with 10-49 employees and micro-enterprises as those with less than 10 employees.[1] When SMEs and micro-enterprises are mentioned together, this means all firms with less than 50 employees.

2.2 Past Export Achievements and The Current Climate

2.2.1 Historical Record

The transformation of the Mauritian economy over the last thirty years from a low productivity, subsistence base to a producer of manufactures for export with an emerging services sector is an impressive developmental achievement. It has built up a significant base of export-related skills, information and institutions, far ahead of neighbouring countries in Africa and is regarded as a candidate for second-tier newly industrialising economy (NIE) status in the 21st century. It had double-digit export growth rates in 1970-92 and by 1996 its manufactured exports per head ($1,022.5) were among the highest in the developing world.[2] Moreover, in relation to its per capita income it had relatively high living standards. A per capita income of $3,800 (1997) places it within the 1998 World Bank *World Development Report's* category of upper-middle income economies and well above the average for Africa ($500) and South Asia ($390). The life expectancy of an average Mauritian was an impressive 72 years in 1996 while the average for Africa was only 53 years and for South Asia was only 51 years.

The causes of Mauritian export success have been well documented by policy makers and others.[3] In the mid-1960s, the country faced many gaps in its initial conditions including a small home market, geographical isolation from international markets and suppliers, and limited industrial experience. Sugar and tourism laid the foundations

[1] The definition was adopted at the request of SMIDO. The logic behind this is explained in Chapter 1.
[2] Calculated from World Bank, World Development Report, 1997.
[3] For a succinct exposition see MEDRC (1997).

for modern Mauritian development by providing a surplus for investment, a pool of managerial skills, and an international country reputation as an exporter. The main engine of structural transformation was export-oriented FDI in EPZs which brought in new technology, managerial skills, marketing contacts and capital. FDI inflows – largely from France, Hong Kong and the UK – averaged $22 million per year in 1985-90 and increased slightly to $23 million in 1991-97.[4] A combination of locational advantages can explain why export-oriented FDI invested in EPZs in Mauritius rather than in South Asia or Africa: cheap and literate labour; preferential access to the European Union market via the Lomé Convention; macroeconomic and political stability relative to competitor locations; a business friendly environment with minimal red tape problems; cost-competitive EPZs; and competitive investment incentives.

Table 2.1: Manufactured Export Performance in 1985-1996

Activity	Values ($millions)	Annual growth rates (%)		% shares
	1996	1985-92	1992-96	1996
Fish & preparations	40.1	–	21.0	3.6
Pearls, precious stones	28.4	15.3	6.0	2.6
Textile yarn, fabrics	80.6	30.9	24.1	7.2
Clothing, accessories (a)	901.9	23.5	7.2	81.1
Toys, sporting goods	10.8	–	0.3	1.0
Gold, jewellery	15.9	34.1	-14.4	1.4
Optical instruments	11.8	–	–	1.1
Watches, clocks	22.6	15.0	-3.5	2.0
Other (b)	n.a	–	-42.4	0.0
Total manufactured exports	1112.0	24.3	8.6	100.0

Source: Based on Lall and Wignaraja (1998).

2.2.2 STRUCTURAL CONSTRAINTS

The early export success, however, was not sustained and several gaps in export performance became apparent in the 1990s. Table 2.1 provides data on recent manufactured export performance in Mauritius (1985-1996). The main findings are as follows:

- There was a deceleration in annual total manufactured export growth in 1992-1996 to about one-third its 1985-1992 rate. This is associated with a sharp fall in clothing (the dominant export) as well as falls in other important exports like textiles, watches and clocks, jewellery, and other manufactured

[4] UN (1998) p. 168.

exports. The slowdown in export growth has had an adverse impact on GDP growth, which fell from 6.2% per year in 1980-90 to 4.9% in 1990-96.

- There is a heavy dependence on a few labour-intensive export products, rendering the country vulnerable to unfavourable national and international developments in those activities. Compared to other developing economies, Mauritius is exceptionally vulnerable with its high dependence on one item (clothing) which has not declined over time.

- There is the virtual absence of more complex industrial goods, either sophisticated consumer or producer goods. It has 'missed the boat' on the semi-conductor assembly boom that drove the growth of Singapore (and later Malaysia) which led to a variety of related electronic and electrical exports. The lack of technological and skill upgrading in the export sector is a significant weakness – it hinders: (i) the realisation of technological spillovers and externalities from complex industries and (ii) the creation of new employment in technology-intensive industries.

Recent studies trace the gaps in export performance in the 1990s to an erosion in the country's locational advantages to FDI (and hence its competitiveness) as well persistent structural weaknesses.[5] The following locational advantages started eroding:

- labour costs had risen significantly, labour productivity declined, and absenteeism rates increased.[6];

- a threat of the elimination of preferential access to the European and US markets with the expiry of the Lomé Agreement and the Multi-Fibre Agreement for textiles;

- residual bureaucratic procedures (particularly on FDI approvals and work permits for expatriate staff) become a barrier to more inward-investment;

- increased competition from lower cost producers in Africa and Asia which had liberalised their entry regulations for FDI and established EPZs;

- inflation starts to increase and with it came relatively high real interest rates and real exchange appreciation.

Some leading Hong Kong and French investors in textiles began to withdraw from Mauritius to other low cost locations like China, Sri Lanka and Bangladesh. About half the foreign-owned firms in a recent enterprise survey are considering, or are in the process of, re-locating to more attractive manufacturing locations.[7] Madagascar

---

[5] See World Bank (1994) and Lall and Wignaraja (1998) for a discussion of these issues.
[6] A recent study found that annual wages in Mauritius manufacturing went up three fold from $1063 to $2998 between 1985 and 1993. The country's 1993 wages were four times higher than those of Sri Lanka and China, three times higher than Bangladesh and twice that of India and Indonesia. In the same study, the enterprise survey reported that 61 per cent of firms felt that the decline in labour productivity was a negative constraint on competitiveness. See Lall and Wignaraja (1998).
[7] See Lall and Wignaraja (1998).

has been a particular beneficiary (due its cheap labour and preferential market access to Europe) and has induced about 40 Mauritius-based enterprises to engage in textile and garment production. Some of these are foreign-owned.

At the same time, several persistent structural weaknesses hindered the upgrading of existing foreign affiliates and the entry of new high skill FDI. These include: inadequate local demand for high technology products arising from a small local market; a lack of reliable suppliers of raw materials, parts and components; and a shortage of technical, engineering and information technology skills for high technology industries. Against this background, the Government of Mauritius began searching for new sources of export growth and SMEs seemed to be an attractive vehicle for future export dynamism.

2.3 The SME and Micro-enterprise Population

2.3.1 THE MAGNITUDE OF SMEs AND MICRO-ENTERPRISES

In Mauritius as in other developing economies, time series information on the size structure of manufacturing activity is difficult to ascertain. The standard data source, Central Statistical Office *Census of Economic Activities* 1992 (referred to as CSO 1994), has separate volumes on small and large establishments engaged in non-primary economic activities. Its coverage of enterprises is impressive and it contains useful data on many indicators of manufacturing activity at industry-level (including value added per person engaged and the average wage bill). However, it is somewhat dated for the purposes of this report and it adopts a restricted definition of small establishments "as those employing 9 or fewer persons inclusive of working proprietors" (CSO 1994, p.1, vol. 1). Typically, studies on SME development in developing economies would view this category of firms as micro-enterprises rather than as small and medium enterprises.[8] Interestingly, CSO (1994) does not provide a breakdown of the size distribution of large establishments, which are defined in aggregate "as those employing 10 or more persons" (CSO 1994, p.1, vol. 2). Manufacturing surveys in developed economies tend to provide a wide range of indicators for different size classes of firms such as <20 employees, 20-99 employees, 100-499 employees and >500 employees.

Given the limitations of CSO (1994), we attempted to make an assessment of the current magnitude and growth of different sizes of firms in the Mauritian manufacturing sector using other data sources and a simple forecasting technique. Table 2.2 provides data on the number of firms, total employment and their growth rates in micro-enterprises (<10 employees), SMEs (10-49 employees) and large firms (>50 employees) in 1992 and 1997. It also combines SMEs and micro-enterprises and provides information for the whole manufacturing sector. The 1992 data are from CSO (1994)

---

[8] See, for instance, Little et al., (1987) and Sengenberger et al., (ed. 1990).

and the database of the Ministry of Industry and Commerce, whereas those for 1997 are a mixture of actual information on SMEs and large firms and our estimates for micro-enterprises.[9] In the absence of recent information, economists commonly forecast trends from historical data on the relevant aggregates.[10] Therefore, the 1997 estimates for micro-enterprises should be regarded as indicative projections rather than real information. Projected data are useful as background inputs into an SME policy planning process but major policy decisions, which affect enterprises, should not be based exclusively on such data.

Table 2.2: Recent Growth of SMEs and Micro-enterprises in Manufacturing, 1992-1997

Firm size group	Number of Firms		Growth rate of firms (% p.a)	Total Employment		Growth rate of employ- ment (% p.a)
	1992	1997	1992-97	1992	1997	1992-97
Large firms (>50 employees)	461	411	-2.3%	97,433	95,078	-0.5%
SMEs (10-49 employees)	487	467	-0.8%	11,856	10,771	-1.9%
Micro-enterprises (<10 employees)	3,932	(c) 4,853	4.3%	14,451	(c) 20,080	6.8%
SMEs and Micro-enterprises (a)	4,419	(b) 5,320	3.8%	26,307	(b) 30,851	3.2%
Total Manufacturing	4,880	5,731	3.3%	123,740	125,929	0.4%

Notes: (a) <50 employees. (b) Addition of actual data on SMEs and forecast data on micro-enterprises. (c) Calculated by extrapolating from 1985-92 compound growth rates.

Source: Our estimates based on data from the Ministry of Industry and Commerce; CSO (1994).

The main findings are as follows:

1. The industrial structure of the Mauritian manufacturing sector exhibits a distinct dualistic pattern, and consists of many small firms and a few large enterprises. According to our estimates, of the 5,320 establishments in 1997, micro-enterprises account for 84.7%, SMEs for 8.1% and large firms for only

[9] To obtain the 1992 data on manufacturing SMEs and micro-enterprises (less than 50 employees), we combined CSO (1994) figures on enterprise numbers and employment in micro-enterprises with Ministry of Industry and Commerce data on SMEs.
[10] We used a simple linear time-trend type forecasting method to obtain the 1997 estimates of establishments and total employment in micro-enterprises (<9 employees). To arrive at the 1997 estimates, yearly compound growth rates were calculated for the variables in 1985-92 (4.3% for establishments and 6.8% for employment) and applied to their 1992 value. Underlying this forecasting method is the assumption that the 1985-92 rate of change applies to the 1993-1997 period. In the absence of appropriate information to adjust the 1985-92 establishment and employment growth rates upwards (or downwards), this is a useful first approximation. The 1985 and 1992 data are from the CSO Census of Economic Activities. Further work is needed to explore the validity of the assumption of constant growth rates.

7.2%.[11] Hence, very small micro-enterprises are the largest group and are followed some way behind by SMEs and large firms.

2. However, this dualism is inverted when it comes to employment shares. Large firms (75.5% of employment) are the dominant source of employment in the manufacturing sector. The number of people employed in large firms (95,078 workers) is nearly five times that of micro-enterprises (20,080 workers) and nearly ten times that of SMEs (10,771 workers).

3. It appears that after many years of growth in the 1970s and 1980s, the number of large firms has declined in the 1990s. At the other extreme of the industrial structure, the number of micro-enterprises has increased. In between, SMEs also seem to have declined in number. The annual growth rates in the number of establishments in 1992-1997 are: large firms (-2.3%), SMEs (-0.8%) and micro-enterprises (4.3%). In part, this growth of micro-enterprises may represent a kind of income substitution whereby ex-large firm employees and redundant civil servants establish new firms to maintain their income.

4. A similar shift seems to be taking place in the structure of employment over time. During 1992-1997, large firms (-1.9%) and SMEs (-0.5%) have witnessed negative employment growth while micro-enterprises seem to have seen positive employment growth (6.8%).

5. These controversial findings should be viewed with caution because the downward trend in establishment numbers and employment for large firms and SMEs are based on actual data while the upward trend for micro-enterprises uses unadjusted forecasts. More primary data collection and empirical research is needed to substantiate these important findings.

---

[11] We were also able to estimate the population of non-primary SMEs and micro-enterprises, which in 1997, was predicted to be 25,761 establishments with about 91,888 people. Manufacturing SMEs and micro-enterprises account for 20.7% of all non-primary establishments and about 33.6% of employment.

Table 2.3: Employment Shares of SMEs in Manufacturing in Different Countries, Latest (a)

Country	Year	% of employment in SMEs
Norway	1985	14.1
Germany	1983	16.0
USA	1982	17.6
UK	1992	27.0
France	1979	28.6
Mauritius	1992	32.1(b)
Korea	1983	33.9
Switzerland	1985	41.2
Taiwan	1981	41.5
Japan	1983	47.7
Italy	1981	55.1

Note: (a) OECD definition of SMEs (<100 employees).
(b) The figure for <50 employees is 21.7%.
Sources: Mauritius (our estimates using CSO 1994 and MOIC data); Taiwan (Wade, 1990); Korea (Amsden, 1989); UK (DTI, 1996); remaining countries (Sengenberger et al., ed. 1990).

A closely related issue is the magnitude of the Mauritian SME and micro-enterprise sector compared with other economies. Table 2.3 provides the latest available information on the employment shares of SMEs in the manufacturing sectors of Mauritius, eight developed economies and two Asian NIEs (Korea and Taiwan). To ensure international comparability of the data, the Table adopts the OECD definition of a small enterprise as one with less than 100 employees.[12] The employment share of SMEs shows considerable variation across the sample countries without any obvious relationship to variables like per capital income, level of industrial development and population.[13] By international standards, Mauritius (32.1%) has quite a respectable SME sector (<100 employees), which is comparable to that of France, UK and Korea.[14] This means that the country has developed a respectable SME base to build on for future industrial and export expansion. Nevertheless, its employment share of SMEs is smaller than those economies – Taiwan, Italy, Japan and Switzerland – which are widely regarded as having the largest and probably most dynamic SME populations in the world.

[12] The Mauritian estimate combined employment data from CSO (1992) for firms with less than 10 employees with data from the Ministry of Industry and Commerce for those with 10-49 employees. The total manufacturing employment figure was the manufacturing totals from both volumes of CSO (1994).
[13] In attempting to explain cross-country differences in SME employment shares, we are inclined to the view of Loveman and Sengenberger (1990): "One has to dig deep into history to understand why and how the structures have developed in this way", (Loveman and Sengenberger, p. 7). This inevitably means looking at a country's initial conditions, factor endowments, enterpreneurial history and government policies.
[14] Defining SMEs and micro-enterprises as those with less than 50 employees results in the share of Mauritian manufacturing employment dropping to 21.7%. This is still quite large by international standards.
[15] See Mead and Liedholm (1998) for the results of SME surveys in several African economies including South Africa and Zimbabwe.

2.3.2 Industry-level Analysis of SMEs

The next issue to consider is the industrial distribution of SMEs in the Mauritian manufacturing sector. Surveys of African developing economies have found that three types of industrial activities have consistently been identified as the most important categories for SMEs and micro-enterprises: *food products, wood and furniture and textiles and clothing*.[15] Food products are widely seen as the ideal entry-level industry for SMEs because of strong local demand, conformity with local consumption patterns, availability of local raw materials and low skill requirements. Wood and furniture are attractive because of local raw materials, carpentry skills and relatively high transport costs that afford protection to local firms. Textiles and clothing have relatively low skill and capital requirements and can cater to local demand but are more import dependent than the other two industries. These surveys estimate that nearly 75% of SMEs and micro-enterprises in most African developing economies are engaged in these three activities. Our estimates suggest that Mauritius conforms to this general pattern but with a somewhat lower figure (51.9%). This may reflect differences in resource endowments, tastes and consumption patterns, skill-levels and degree of trade openness.

We are able to illuminate aspects of SME development at industry-level using data from the Ministry of Industry and Commerce (comparable figures were not available on micro-enterprises). These are:

Table 2.4: Size Structure of Firms and Employment in the Manufacturing Sector, 1997

Industry	All Firms: Number of firms	Employment	10-49 employees: (a) % of all firms	% of all emp.
Food	109	10,301	62.4	12.9
Textiles	52	5,517	55.8	12.9
Clothing	332	67,495	33.1	4.0
Footwear & leather	23	1,928	52.2	11.2
Wood & furniture	43	1,673	81.4	44.0
Precision equipment (b)	16	1,480	50.0	11.4
Jewellery	21	1,710	47.6	18.3
Other	282	15,655	69.1	29.2
Total manufacturing	878	105,829	56.6	10.2
Values	878	105,829	467	10,771

Note: (a) Defined as SMEs for this study (excludes micro-enterprises with <10 employees).
(b) Professional/scientific measuring equipment & optical goods.
Source: Our estimates based on data from the Ministry of Industry and Commerce.

---

[15] See Mead and Liedholm (1998) for the results of SME surveys in several African economies including South Africa and Zimbabwe.

(1) *The number of SMEs by industry-membership.* In 1997 there were 467 SMEs in the manufacturing sector in Mauritius (i.e., enterprises with between 10-49 employees). Textiles and clothing are the dominant industry (29.8% of the number of SMEs). This is followed some way behind by food products (14.6%), wood and furniture (7.5%), footwear and leather products (2.6%), jewellery (2.1%) and professional equipment (1.7%). There is also a large miscellaneous category called other manufacturing, which makes up 41.7%. This needs further analysis. However, the mission does not have additional information in this instance.

(2) *The share of SMEs in manufacturing establishment numbers and employment.* Table 2.4 provides data on size structure of employment in the manufacturing sector in 1997 for three groups of firms: 10-49 employees (SMEs), 50-99 employees (large firms) and above 100 employees (very large firms).16 Taken together, these three size groups accounted for 878 firms and 105,829 workers in 1997. The data suggest a highly skewed pattern of establishments and employment by firm size within individual industries. The striking fact is that SMEs account for a relatively high proportion of establishments in most industries (averaging 56.6%) but relatively small employment shares (averaging 10.2%). The only exceptions

50-99 employees:		>100 employees:	
% of all firms	% of all emp.	% of all firms	% of all emp.
10.1	8.1	27.5	79.8
19.2	14.4	25.0	72.7
18.7	6.5	48.2	89.5
26.1	19.3	21.7	69.6
9.3	18.4	9.3	37.6
18.8	16.4	31.3	72.2
28.6	28.1	23.8	53.6
19.1	24.0	11.7	46.8
17.8	10.6	29.0	79.3
156	11,168	255	83,910

are wood and furniture and, to a lesser extent, jewellery and textiles and clothing. In contrast, very large firms (above 100 employees) account for under one-third of establishments but nearly four-fifths of employment in most industries. In between these extremes, large firms (50-99 employees) are relatively unimportant in terms of establishments or employment.

It would be useful to analyse changes in the size structure of the number of establishments and employment over time in Mauritius. However, no data seems to be collected locally on the births and deaths of new firms. This is a major gap in current data collection and enterprise surveys.

2.4 Recent Trends in SME Manufactured Exports

Having looked at the magnitude of the SME population and its industrial distribution, we focus on SME export performance. A useful way of looking at the manufactured export performance of SMEs is by the trade and industrial policy regime, which governs the market-orientation of different enterprises. These regimes will be discussed in more detail in chapter 4, dealing with the policy framework for SME development. Suffice to note that the EPZ regime provides incentives and infrastructure that encourages export production while the non-EPZ regime emphasises domestic market production. No information is available on the export performance of micro-enterprises but our impression is that such firms are rarely engaged in exports. Table 2.5 categorises the total population of 467 SMEs (10-49 employees) according to their trade orientation and provides data for 1997 on number of firms, employment, exports, employees/firm and exports/firm for each group.

Taken together, in 1997 the 467 EPZ and non-EPZ SMEs generated manufactured exports worth $23.5 million and 10,771 jobs. This represents a useful contribution to foreign exchange earnings and employment creation in the Mauritian economy. There are some important differences in the performance of the two groups of SMEs.

Table 2.5: EPZ and Non-EPZ SMEs in the Manufacturing Sector in 1997 (a)

	Number of firms	Total employment	Total exports ($ m)	Employees per firm	Exports per firm ($)
All SMEs	467	10,771	23.5	23.1	50,321.2
Of which:					
EPZ SMEs	153	3,802	20.4	24.8	133,333.3
Non-EPZ SMEs	314	6,969	3.1	22.2	9,872.6

Note: (a) SMEs are defined as those with 10-49 employees only. This excludes micro-enterprises with less than 10 employees

Source: Our estimates from based on data from Ministry of Industry and Commerce.

The number of non-EPZ SMEs (314) is more than double that of EPZ SMEs (153 firms). They also provide more overall employment than the EPZ SMEs – manufactured employment in non-EPZ SMEs (6,969 workers) is almost double that of EPZ SMEs (3,802 workers)

At the same time, non-EPZ SMEs appear less efficient than the EPZ SMEs.

- One aspect of this is *jobs per firm*. The former had an average of 22.2 jobs per firm in 1997 compared with 24.8 jobs for the latter.

- Far more serious is the gap in *export performance*. The larger number of non-EPZ SMEs generates fewer exports, overall and per firm, than EPZ SMEs. The value of manufactured exports in non-EPZ SMEs is only 15.4% of EPZ SMEs. In addition, the value of exports per firm is much smaller in non-EPZ SMEs ($9,873) compared to EPZ SMEs ($133,333).

Thus, the EPZ SME sector seems to be more efficient in terms of generating exports and employment than the non-EPZ SME sector. The next two sub-sections examine the industry-level exporting behaviour of SMEs in the EPZ and non-EPZ sectors.

2.4.1 EPZ SME Exports

Table 2.6 provides annual data on the value of manufactured exports in SMEs ($ million) in the EPZ sector in 1995-1997 by industry and the cumulative shares of

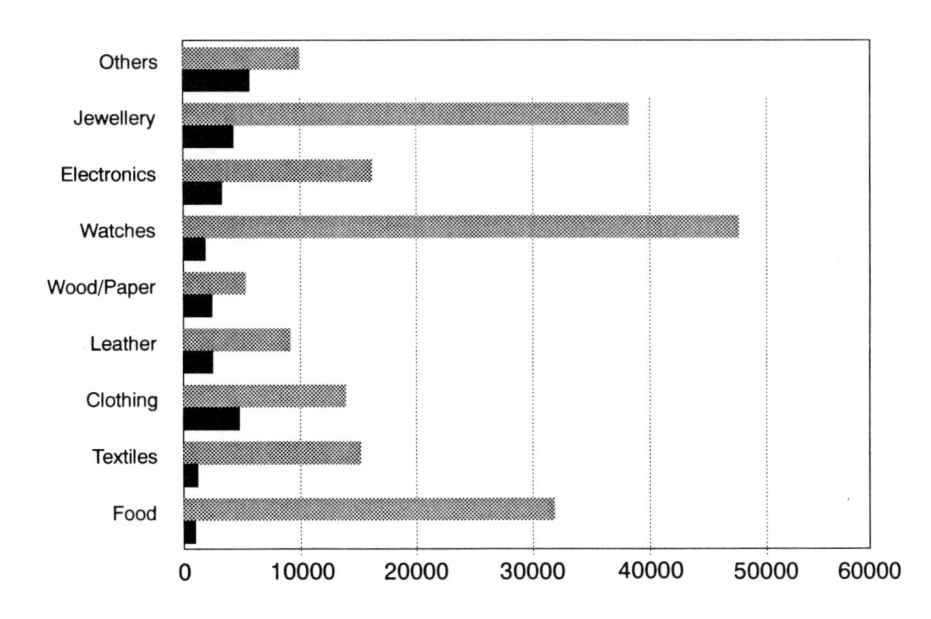

Fig 2.1   Exports/employee in the EPZ, $ 1997

different industries during 1995-1997. This data is classified according to skill intensity into low and high skill industries.[17] The former is based on simple labour skills and technologies and the latter on more complex skills and technologies. The value of manufactured exports from EPZ SMEs was relatively stable during 1995-1997 and averaged $21.6 million per year in this period. The following points can be made about the structure of manufactured exports from EPZ SMEs:

- The majority of such exports (96.6%) consist of low skill activities, which are based on simple labour skills and technologies.

- A single low skill export (clothing) dominates EPZ SME exports and alone made-up 42.8% of cumulative EPZ SME exports.

- Three other low skill activities – flowers, jewellery and wood/paper products – accounted for another 15.1%.

Table 2.6: Manufactured Exports in Large Firms and SMEs in the EPZ, 1995-1997

	EPZ Large Firms	
	Manufactured exports ($ m)	Growth rate (% p.a)
	1997	1995-1997
Low Skill:		
Food	44.3	-10.6
Flowers	0.0	n.a.
Textile Yarn	44.5	-12.3
Clothing	851.3	5.0
Leather & Footwear	11.5	-5.5
Wood & Paper Products	1.0	-0.3
Jewellery & Related Articles	37.8	-1.4
Toys & Carnival Articles	5.8	-28.4
Others	7.1	-36.6
High Skill:		
Optical goods	9.6	-15.0
Watches and Clocks	7.0	-47.7
Electric & Electronic Products	6.8	1.9
Total Exports	1026.7	0.7

Notes: (a) Compound growth rate.
Rupee figures converted into $ at official rates given in the IMF *International Financial Statistics*.
Source: Our estimates from based on data from Ministry of Industry and Commerce, 1998

[17] In line with international practice, the average wage in US manufacturing industries was used to classify industries in low and high skill activities. Industries above the manufacturing average were classed as high skill and those below were low skill. See Wignaraja (1998).

- Apart from these, there were relatively small shares of food products, textile yarn, leather and footwear, and toys that together accounted for 6.1%. There was also a large category of miscellaneous manufactures.
- In contrast, high skill activities only accounted for 3.4% of cumulative EPZ SME exports. These consisted of very small shares of watches and clocks (2.3%) and electrical and electronics products (1.1%)

The previous section showed that EPZ SMEs had higher exports per firm than non-EPZ firms in 1997. We can further investigate the export dynamism of EPZ SMEs by comparing their performance with those of large EPZ firms using three sets of indicators:

First, *manufactured export growth rates* (in current $) for 1995-1997 which show how fast overall EPZ SME exports and industry-level SME EPZ exports are changing relative to those of large firms. Table 2.6 also provides manufactured export growth rates for

EPZ Small and Medium Enterprise				
Manufactured exports ($ m)			% of cumulative total	Growth rate (% p.a)
1995	1996	1997	1995-1997	1995-1997
0.9	0.4	0.2	2.2	-56.3
1.6	1.2	1.0	5.8	-20.9
0.7	0.5	0.3	2.3	-29.4
7.5	10.8	9.4	42.8	12.5
0.0	0.1	0.1	0.3	23.6
0.9	0.9	0.9	4.1	1.9
0.4	1.9	1.2	5.2	80.7
0.4	0.5	0.0	1.3	–
8.7	7.0	5.4	32.5	-21.2
0.0	0.0	0.0	0.0	0.0
0.04	0.0	1.4	2.3	500.4
0.1	0.1	0.5	1.1	150.1
21.0	23.4	20.4	100.0	-1.5

EPZ SMEs and large firms by industry. Total EPZ SME manufactured exports had a negative growth rate (-1.5% p.a) during 1995-1997 compared with a low but positive growth rate for EPZ large firms (0.7% p.a). The weak performance of total SME manufactured exports could be due to negative growth rates in several core activities (other manufactured products, food, flowers and textile yarn), the total decline of toys, and slow positive growth in wood/paper products. Three other items (jewellery, watches and clocks and electric and electronic items) recorded high positive growth rates. But, as these were from a very small base, they had little influence on the overall manufactured export growth rate of SMEs.

Interestingly, clothing (the single largest SME export) had a respectable positive export growth rate. The large firm performance is more uneven than in the case of SMEs: only two activities recorded positive export growth rates (clothing and electrical and electronics products). The remainder had negative growth rates.

Table 2.7: Shares of SMEs and Large Firms in EPZ Exports, 1997

Sector	SMEs	Large Firms
Low Skill:		
Food	0.4	99.6
Flowers	100.0	0.0
Textile Yarn	0.8	99.2
Clothing	1.1	98.9
Leather & Footwear	0.6	99.4
Wood & Paper Products	47.6	52.4
Jewellery & Related Articles	3.0	97.0
Toys & Carnival Articles	0.0	100.0
Others	43.2	56.8
High Skill		
Optical Goods	0.0	100.0
Watches & Clocks	16.9	83.1
Electric & Electronic Products	7.0	93.0
Total EPZ Exports	1.9	98.1

Second, *manufactured exports per employee for EPZ SMEs and large firms within the same industry*, which can be taken as a simple proxy for labour productivity in the manufacturing export sector.[18] Figure 2.1 shows exports per employee in EPZ SMEs and large firms in nine industrial branches in 1997. It is impressive that, EPZ SMEs have lower ratios of exports per employee than large firms do in all nine industrial branches. In the case of total EPZ exports, SME exports per employee are only 27.5%

[18] The lack of published information on value added per employee and capital per employee in SMEs and large firms prevented the use of more accurate measures of productivity in this report.

of that for large firms. This aggregate figure masks considerable inter-industrial variation between SMEs and large firms. The ratio of SME to large firm exports per employee is lowest in food (2.9%), watches and clocks (3.6%) textiles (6.2%) and jewellery (11.1%). It is highest in other manufactured items (54.2%) and wood/paper products (43.5%). In between fall clothing (32.1%), leather and footwear (25.1%), electrical and electronics items (21.0%).

Third, the *shares of SMEs and large firms in industry-level and overall manufactured exports*, which represents a way of gauging the importance of different enterprise size groups in national exports. Table 2.7 provides data on the respective contributions of SMEs and large firms to EPZ exports in 1997. SMEs (1.9%) make a negligible contribution to total EPZ exports compared with large firms (98.1%). However, SMEs seem to produce all the EPZ's flower exports and significant shares of EPZ exports of wood/paper products (47.6%), other manufactured exports (43.2%) and watches and clocks (16.9%). SMEs contribute little to the remaining EPZ exports (including clothing, the leading national export). Thus, with a few exceptions, large firms seem to dominate EPZ exports.

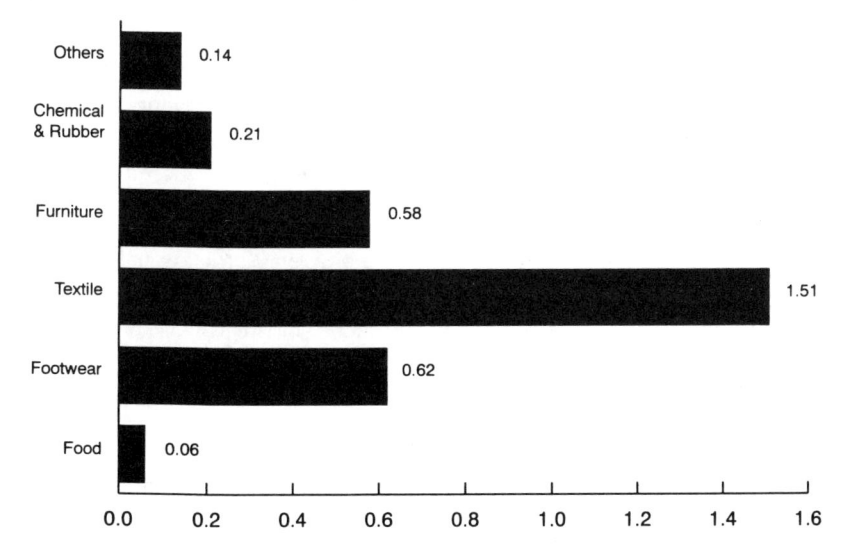

Fig 2.2: Non-EPZ SME Exports

Category	Value
Others	0.14
Chemical & Rubber	0.21
Furniture	0.58
Textile	1.51
Footwear	0.62
Food	0.06

2.4.2 Non-EPZ SME Exports

Previous studies have noted that non-EPZ SMEs "are not major exporters of manufactures and have few linkages with EPZ firms"(World Bank, 1994, p.v). Most non-EPZ SMEs produce entirely for the domestic market. A few non-EPZ SMEs might have made an occasional export in response to an export order but usually this was not sustained. A survey undertaken by SMIDO for the Commonwealth mission indicated that out of 314 non-EPZ SMEs in 1997 only about 26 enterprises were engaged in exports (8.3%). The total value of exports from these 26 firms increased from $1.7 million to $2.4 million between 1995 and 1996 and still further to $3.1 million in 1997. This is clearly a healthy start. Inspite of this progress, even the 1997 value of exports from non-EPZ SMEs remains small as a ratio of either EPZ SME exports (1.9%) or total EPZ exports (0.3%). Figure 2.2 provides a breakdown of non-EPZ SME exports in 1997. Nearly half of these exports consist of textiles ($1.5 million). Footwear ($ 0.62 million) and furniture ($0.58 million) also account for reasonable shares. The remainder (food, chemicals and rubber and other manufactures) is negligible.

2.5 Conclusions

The Chapter highlighted many aspects of the magnitude and dynamism of SMEs and micro-enterprise in the Mauritian manufacturing sector in the 1990s. At the request of SMIDO, the study adopted the following definitions: SMEs (10-49 employees), micro-enterprises (<10 employees) and large firms (>50 employees). When SMEs and micro-enterprises are mentioned together, this means all firms with less than 50 employees.

The most significant findings are:

- The industrial structure of the Mauritian manufacturing sector has a distinct dualistic pattern made up of many small firms and a few large firms. Our estimates suggest that of the 5,320 manufacturing establishments in 1997, 84.7% were micro-enterprises, 8.1% were SMEs and 7.2% were large firms. The relatively few large firms account for the bulk of manufacturing employment.

- After many years of expansion in the 1970s and 1980s, the annual average growth rate of the number of large firms (-2.3%) and SMEs (-0.8%) has declined in 1992-1997 while that of micro-enterprises (4.3%) has increased. These trends should be viewed with caution because the figures for large firms and SMEs use actual data while those for micro-enterprises are unadjusted forecasts.

- In 1997, there were 467 SMEs, which collectively made a useful contribution to the Mauritian foreign exchange earnings by generating a total of $23.5 million worth of manufactured exports.

- However, as a group EPZ SMEs have been much more efficient in generating exports than non-EPZ SMEs. The value of manufactured exports from EPZ SMEs ($20.4 million) is over six times that of non-EPZ SMEs ($3.1 million) in 1997.

- EPZ SMEs (1.9%) made a negligible contribution to total EPZ exports in 1997 compared with large EPZ firms (98.1%). The aggregate figure masks the fact that SMEs seem to produce all the EPZ's flower exports and useful shares of EPZ exports of wood/paper products, other manufactured exports and watches and clocks.

- Total EPZ SME manufactured exports had a negative growth rate (-1.5% p.a.) in 1995-1997 compared with a low but positive growth rate for EPZ large firms (0.7%).

- The weak performance of EPZ SME exports is due to negative growth in several core activities (other manufactured products, food, flowers and textile yarn), the total decline of toys, and slow positive growth in wood/paper products. Three other items (jewellery, watches and clocks and electric and electronic items) had high positive growth. But, as these were from a small base, they had little influence on the overall export growth rate of SMEs. Interestingly, clothing (the single largest SME export) had respectable positive export growth.

- EPZ SMEs had lower ratios of exports per employee than large firms in most industrial branches in 1997. This simple and crude measure of labour productivity suggests that productivity in SMEs lags behind large firms in the EPZ.

- Survey estimates suggest that most non-EPZ SMEs produce entirely for the domestic market. Out of a total of 314 non-EPZ SMEs, only about 26 were engaged in exports in 1997. These firms exported very small shares of the country's exports of textiles, footwear and furniture.

- No data was available on the manufactured export performance of micro-enterprises but they were believed to be nearly all domestic market-oriented.

3 Evaluation of SME Capabilities

3.1 Introduction

This chapter aims to evaluate the capabilities of the SME sector in developing export competitiveness. It builds on an enterprise survey of Mauritian SMEs in textiles, printing and publishing and IT. Both face-to-face interviews and a questionnaire were used to collect the requisite information (see Appendix 1).

Capabilities are identified in relation to a) competences in marketing, design, use of technology and human resource management; b) strategy: a company's choice of target markets and its positioning within those markets; and c) managerial characteristics: head of the enterprise's commitment, and his or her orientation and attitude to exporting (see Appendix 2).

3.2 Competences

Competences are defined as capabilities at the functional level of an enterprise. Here, we are looking at the understanding and use of the various elements of the marketing mix, the use of design and technology and the management of the human resource. These are considered in relation to each of the three industry sectors surveyed.

Obviously, functional level activities should primarily serve to implement strategy. A discussion of the capabilities of SMEs to develop appropriate strategies will follow this section.

3.2.1 MARKETING

Marketing capabilities at the functional level imply the ability to use effectively the elements of the marketing mix. Specifically, these relate to decisions on product, price, promotion and distribution.

3.2.1.1 Textiles

Product – Ten of the seventeen firms surveyed are producing casualwear, predominantly T-shirts and shorts from cotton weave and cotton jersey. Two companies are specialising in baby and childrenswear, one in swimwear, two in lingerie and one in woven labels. Another is a tailor producing uniforms for hotels and some custom suits for men and women.

Samples of products from eight companies were seen. Apart from two firms, product quality is low relative to European expectations. One manufacturer commented that his products were too high quality for the domestic market, but in our view they would not be competitive in sophisticated American or European markets. Design content is minimal and products lack differentiation. The same T-shirts and shorts are available everywhere in the world. The range of fabrics used is limited.

Product ranges tend to be far too broad leading to very short production runs. The inclination is to spread risk by producing lots of different types and styles of garments, rather than specialising and focusing on specific customer segments. Only two companies have a clear picture of their target consumer. Understanding of the concept of a brand was lacking in most cases.

Pricing – Most companies were trying to compete on price and calculated price on the basis of cost-plus. This method calculates the cost of inputs and adds a predetermined profit margin. The approach is consistent with low value-add, but the relatively high labour costs in Mauritius, compared with increasingly important competitors such as those in Sri Lanka and Vietnam, precludes this as a useful competitive strategy. Higher quality, differentiated products, would enable the use of a perceived-value pricing strategy – where prices are set on the basis of the value perceived by customers, and which invariably delivers higher profits.

Promotion – The table below shows the use of various promotional tools by the thirteen textile companies who responded to our questionnaire.

Table 3.1: Use of Promotional Tools in the Textile Industry

	Number of companies			
	Use extensively	Use moderately	Hardly use	Don't use
Trade fairs	2	2	1	8
Advertising	1	5	1	6
Brochures/literature	1	3	1	8
Professional marketing services	2	1	2	8
Personal selling	7	2	2	2
Direct marketing/direct mail (a)	5	1	1	4
Web page/email (b)	0	3	0	9

Notes: (a) Two respondents left this question blank.
(b) One respondent left this question blank.

Trade fairs are used extensively by both large and small firms throughout the world. They provide an opportunity for sellers to demonstrate their products, to meet buyers face-to-face, and to gain competitor intelligence.

The major forms of ***advertising*** are TV or radio commercials, or print, in either consumer or trade press. Most SMEs would find advertising in trade press the most affordable and effective.

Brochures and other forms of corporate literature, such as clothing tags and labels, and product guides are a cost-effective way for companies to make customers aware of their product range, as well as to support the brand proposition.

Professional marketing services are delivered by marketing consultancies and can range from developing a strategic marketing plan to implementing promotional activities, such as advertising or designing a brochure, providing information on markets, fostering contacts with potential buyers, or acting as agents.

Personal selling is a promotional method that utilises a traditional salesforce to identify individual customers and make sales.

Direct marketing is a means of communicating directly with targeted customers using a range of techniques of which specially designed mailings and telephone selling are the most appropriate for the SME sector. Increasingly in business-to-business markets, **relationship marketing** can be adopted, whereby the seller develops a close interpersonal relationship with individual customers through the use of activities such as hospitality, regular direct telephone or email contact, joint product development, etc.

Increasingly a **web site** is considered to be essential for any business, but is particularly affordable for the smaller enterprise. **Email** accessibility, both to maintain relationships with existing customers and to receive enquiries from new customers is also becoming a critical tool.

Small businesses need to maximise their use of promotional tools, utilising as wide a range as is economically feasible. M use is made of the major promotional tools by our survey respondents. There is an overemphasis on personal selling, which is the most expensive tool, whilst the most targeted and cost-effective approaches, which are also the ones that are most appropriate for export initiatives, such as direct marketing and the internet are virtually ignored.

Marketing expenditure as a percentage of turnover is stated by nine companies as follows:

Table 3.2: Marketing Expenditure as a Percentage of Turnover in the Textile Industry

Company 1	0.00%
Company 2	0.00%
Company 3	0.57%
Company 4	0.63%
Company 5	1.00%
Company 6	1.79%
Company 7	2.00%
Company 8	3.70%
Company 9	0.42%
Average	**1.12%**

These figures are low by any industry standard and would cast doubt on the respondents' assertions of "extensive use" of promotional tools.

Distribution – The majority of garment manufacturers are making sales directly to retailers or consumers. Only four use agents and five use wholesalers. Since success in exporting is largely a result of developing contractual relationships with agents and distributors, SMEs in Mauritius are poorly placed to develop exporting capabilities.

Access to overseas markets was cited as a common barrier to exporting with only one company having any formal ongoing arrangements with agents or distributors. For another company, export orders were achieved when visitors from Réunion and Seychelles, on a combination buying/holiday trip, saw their products in a retail outlet. Yet another company uses door-to-door salesmen to make local sales, but its export sales depend on overseas buyers making the first contact.

Overall, the strategic importance of developing channels to market appears to be largely unrecognised within the SME textile sector in Mauritius and the process, if it happens at all, tends to be ad hoc and reactive.

3.2.1.2 Printing and Publishing

Product – The range and type of products produced by companies in this sector is significantly less homogeneous than those within textiles. Two of the firms we interviewed and another five who responded to our questionnaire could be described as jobbing printers. These companies produce relatively simple corporate stationery such as letterheads, brochures, posters, menus, plus a limited amount of packaging. They operate on a reactive basis, responding to the demands of their customers, without any attempt to specialise in a specific product area. This also means that print runs tend to be short.

Overall, the quality is low, with one company in particular producing exceptionally low quality output. However, it should be borne in mind that print quality is highly dependent on technology and the two companies in this category that we observed are using mostly outdated equipment.

Another printing company has chosen to specialise in print for the textile industry. This includes labels and tags, swing tickets, adhesive stickers and some stationery. With a clearly defined market, this company works closely with its customers to determine product specification and its quality is consistent with the needs of the market. It can be considered a non-exporting enterprise as only 0.02% of its sales derive from overseas, specifically Madagascar, and these sales are derived from sub-contracting arrangements by Mauritian firms.

Only one company we saw in the traditional printing sector was operating at the high-end. This firm produces books, magazines and brochures of exceptionally high quality, using state-of-the-art technology. Currently, 22% of its output goes abroad, but, in our view, this is the only traditional printer that has the potential to become a major exporter. That it has not done so to date appears to be owing to internal management problems.

All of these firms, even the smallest, have developed some degree of computer-based pre-press capability.

Of the three other companies we interviewed in the printing and publishing sector, two are wholly owned by French parent companies and operate as pre-press and pre-media production units. Neither initiate any of their own sales and have no intention of doing so.

The last is a single entrepreneur who has catalogued the total Mauritian legal framework, authored it on to one CD-Rom and targeted lawyers. His gross profit margins are so high that he said he is embarrassed to tell us what they are. Future plans of his include producing a CD of Mauritian fauna and flora. This is a very simple but brilliant idea, using low-cost technology, and although this particular businessman has no personal inclination to extend his business overseas, it is an example of how a good product idea, targeted at a clearly definable market, can form the basis of a successful domestic and export business.

Pricing – All of the traditional printers stated that they were competing heavily on price, and this is consistent with the low value-add that most of them were demonstrating. Printing tends to be very price sensitive and a sufficient contribution to fixed costs is usually achieved through producing very high volumes. One company complained that predatory pricing by large printing houses is a major problem. Another cited "unfair competition", although did not elaborate on this.

Although the one company producing very high quality print is better able to charge premium prices, profits from exports are severely reduced by the cost of air freight. When asked how significant an obstacle is the cost of air and sea freight, all of the printing companies rated it at least three, on a scale of 1 to 5, where 5 is the greatest obstacle, and more than half rated it at 5.

In the case of the two repro houses, (those involved in pre-press and pre-media) pricing appeared to be determined by the parent company on the basis of cost. Here, the objective is to minimise costs through the effective management of the production process.

Only the CD authoring company was able to use a perceived pricing strategy, where price is related to the value perceived by the customer, rather than based on cost-plus or competitor pricing.

Promotion -Eleven companies in the printing and publishing sector responded to the question on use of promotional tools.

Table 3.3: Use of Promotional Tools in the Printing and Publishing Industry

	Number of companies			
	Use extensively	Use moderately	Hardly use	Don't use
Trade fairs	1	3	0	7
Advertising	0	7	0	4
Brochures/literature	1	3	1	6
Professional marketing services	1	2	1	7
Personal selling	10	0	0	0
Direct marketing/direct mail	4	4	0	3
Web page/email	0	2	1	8

As with textiles, personal selling is the promotional tool used most extensively. It is especially surprising that six companies do not use brochures at all, particularly as these would act as an example of the work they can produce, and also that eight companies make no use of a web page or email, when most of the firms already have the computer infrastructure in place. Overall, the profile of promotion is similar to the textile industry, with relatively little use being made of the total range of tools.

Marketing expenditure as a percentage of turnover was declared by six companies as:

Table 3.4: Marketing Expenditure as a Percentage of Turnover in the Printing and Publishing Industry

Company 1	4.50%
Company 2	0.68%
Company 3	0.11%
Company 4	0.00%
Company 5	4.29%
Company 6	0.26%
Average	**1.64%**

Company 1 makes most use of all the promotional tools, whilst Company 5 is the CD-Rom company, operating as a direct marketing organisation. Overall, the spend on marketing is very low indeed.

Distribution – Of thirteen companies questioned, seven are making 100% of their sales direct to end-users, most of these being corporate clients. The two French-owned companies are also making sales directly to the parent companies, 100% in one case, and 90% in the other. Only four companies are using agents, wholesalers and retailers to help with their distribution. Two of these are active exporters, exemplifying a known correlation between export capability and use of intermediaries.

3.2.1.3 IT

Product – Activities that fall within the IT sector are even more diverse than in printing and publishing. Of the five companies researched, the following products or services are being offered:

Table 3.5:   Products and Services Offered by Respondents in the IT Industry

Company 1	Computer hardware
Company 2	Call centre
Company 3	Computer hardware, consumables for photocopiers, projects (software and services)
Company 4	Software programming
Company 5	Software development

Three are active exporters. The firm engaged in software programming was established as a wholly-owned development department of a UK parent, utilising the lower labour costs of Mauritius. The fifth is a company set up expressly to develop software for the Mauritian sugar cane industry.

Because of the diversity of "product" and the limited size of the sample, it is difficult to comment on how companies are using this element of the marketing mix. However, consideration of the development of the IT industry in Europe and the US shows a shift from the dominance of hardware, through software, to IT services. As computer hardware diffuses through the corporate and individual population, the price comes down and added value begins to be represented by software. This, in turn, becomes more commoditised and is replaced as a value-add proposition by the delivery of IT services.

The development of one company in the sample demonstrates this shift and indicates a good understanding of market forces. Company 3 started by importing and selling Olivetti computers on the domestic market. This proved unprofitable and sourcing of hardware was switched to buying PC-clones from Asian countries. Financial losses forced them to review their product strategy and they realised they lacked market focus. The company is now divided into three business units, one of which – IT projects – is recognised as offering the biggest growth opportunity. The two other units should provide the means to invest in the development of the projects business. In due course, they intend to create a reseller network to deliver computer hardware and photocopier consumables, so that they can focus on their business-to-business activities.

Small and medium enterprises are well suited to the IT industry. Competition appears not to be intense, and with careful strategy choices, IT represents a substantial opportunity for SMEs in Mauritius. This will be discussed later in more depth.

Pricing – No information was available on how these IT companies price their products or services. Pricing for hardware and software is generally very competitive and prices are likely to be determined on a cost-plus basis with very low margins. The pricing of software development and services will be based partly on the cost of labour, but with the additional opportunity to adopt a perceived value pricing strategy.

Promotion – Statistical figures on promotional expenditure as a percentage of sales were available for only Company 1, selling computer hardware, 3.45%. Data on use of promotional tools was available for only two companies.

Table 3.6: Use of Promotional Tools in the IT Industry

	Number of companies			
	Use extensively	Use moderately	Hardly use	Don't use
Trade fairs	1			1
Advertising	2			
Brochures/literature	1	1		
Professional marketing services			1	1
Personal selling	1			1
Direct marketing/direct mail	1	1		
Web page/email	1	1		

Overall, these two companies are making more extensive use of all the tools compared to textiles and printing and publishing.

It was clear from our in-depth interviews that Companies 4 and 5, with their captive markets, have no need to use forms of promotion other than developing and maintaining good customer relationships. Company 3 stated that they use no promotion as word of mouth has been sufficient for them so far. However, if they wish to further penetrate overseas markets, they must develop a promotional strategy.

Distribution – Company 1 makes full use of the range of distribution channels available, selling 50% direct to end-users, 20% each to wholesalers and retailers, and 10% through agents. As mentioned before, Company 3 is planning to integrate forward by setting up its own reseller network, retaining some of the profits and reducing some of the costs of distribution. For the remaining companies, distribution in this sense has no relevance.

3.2.2 DESIGN

Although design is generally considered to be a subset of marketing in its role in product development and promotion, here it is given prominence because of its potential to add value. This is particularly relevant to the textile industry, although design is also important in printing and publishing. For the IT industry, graphic design can play a part in promotion, but apart from software design which is not considered here, design is not an integral element of its proposition. IT, therefore, is excluded from this analysis.

The quantitative measurements we can apply to SMEs are the number designers used. This gives an indication of the company's commitment to design, but can in no way measure the quality of design output. To assess this, where possible we have visually observed companies' products.

3.2.2.1 Textiles

Three textile companies use no designers at all. Interestingly, two produce babywear, so they may assume that this type of product does not require a professional design input. One of these companies was personally interviewed and product observed, and it is our view that, although the babywear is functional and looks presentable, good design content is noticeably lacking.

Two garment manufacturers each employed one full-time, but untrained, designer. Neither of these were interviewed personally, so we cannot assess the quality of the design.

In order to rank companies by their use of designers, we have designed a crude scoring system as follows:

Table 3.7: Scoring System for Design

Each untrained designer used	1 points
Each trained designer used	2 points
Each part-time designer	1 point
Each full-time designer	2 points
Each freelance designer	1 point
Each in-house designer	2 points
Each design consultant	3 points

So, for example, a company using 1 full-time, in-house trained designer, will score 6, made up of 2 points for the designer being full-time, 2 points for the designer being trained, and 2 points for the designer being in-house. A firm using 1 freelance trained designer will score 3 points, made up of 1 point for the designer being freelance and 2 points for the designer being trained. This scoring assumes that the use of full-timers represents more of a commitment than using part-timers, and using in-house designers more of a commitment than using freelance.

Figure 3.1: The Use of Designers in Sixteen Textile Companies

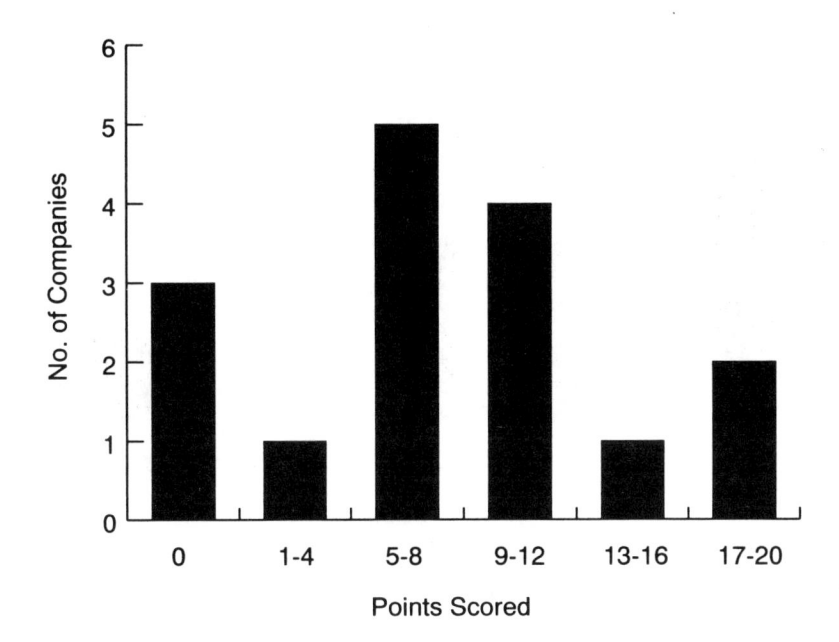

[Bar chart: No. of Companies vs Points Scored]
- 0: 3
- 1-4: 1
- 5-8: 5
- 9-12: 4
- 13-16: 1
- 17-20: 2

It can be seen that two companies are making considerably more use of design than the others. One of these enterprises was visited by the mission and it is clear from seeing their products that their use of design has added significant value. This company has been successful in selling into European markets, but interestingly, the other is a non-exporter. Not having seen the products of this second company, it is impossible to say whether their use of design is sufficiently good for them to be competitive in sophisticated markets.

Apart from these two, quality of design was most pronounced in the two companies producing specialist products, swimwear and lingerie. Another firm was using a designer to produce only surface designs for T-shirts, although these were interesting and effective. Elsewhere, designers appeared to be designing functional clothing, but with little flair or originality.

3.2.2.2 Printing and Publishing

Using the same scoring method, the use of designers in the six printing and publishing enterprises for which we have data, is shown below.

A similar skewed distribution to the textile industry can be seen, although the differential between the minimum and maximum use of design is greater. This is accounted for by the high-end printer described earlier employing 6 trained designers,

Figure 3.2: The Use of Designers in Eight Printing and Publishing Companies

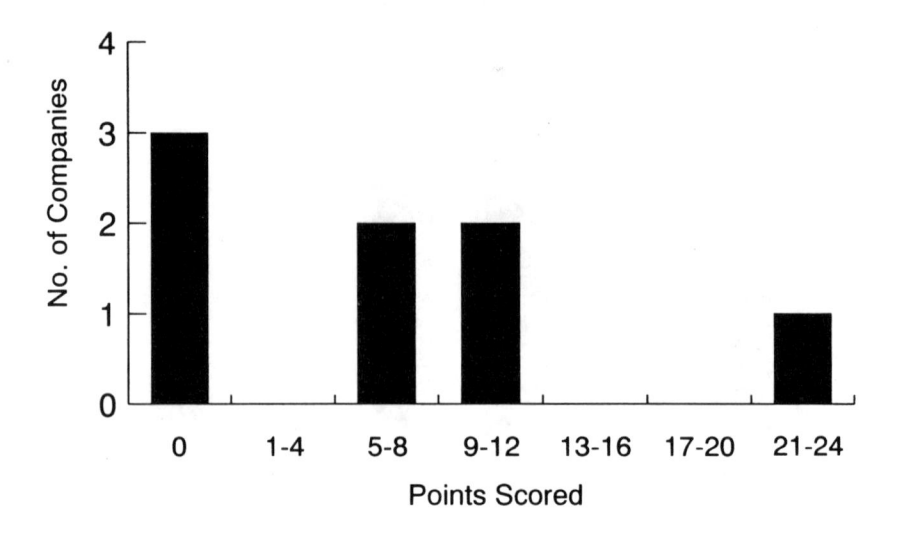

[Bar chart: No. of Companies vs Points Scored. 0: 3 companies; 1-4: 0; 5-8: 2; 9-12: 2; 13-16: 0; 17-20: 0; 21-24: 1]

2 full-time in-house and 4 freelance. Their effectiveness is evident in the quality of the output produced by this company.

3.2.3 TECHNOLOGY

Whilst it is generally accepted that companies need to make the best use of current technology to become or remain competitive, the nature of that technology is changing. In many industry sectors, the sources of competitive advantage are shifting away from traditional capital equipment intensity and towards the effective use of processes, people and information.

In each of the three sectors we studied, the nature, role and exploitation of technology differs considerably.

3.2.3.1 Textiles

World Bank (1994) identifies some critical issues relating to the competitiveness of garment manufacturers in the EPZ:

- Although around half of firms in the apparel industry operate in the low-end segment where price is the major source of competitive advantage, relatively high labour costs make this market position untenable.
- Upgrading into mid-market products is a viable strategy, but is dependent on enhancing design, quality and delivery.

- Relevant technologies include: CAD/CAM systems, computerised sewing/stitching machinery, automated cloth-handling systems, automation of post-CMT processes, group work systems, effective quality control, management information and production control systems.

The study identifies that in every relevant technology Mauritian firms are lagging behind developed countries. Competing in international markets requires levels of technology that can deliver continuous improvements in product quality and design, productivity, flexible manufacturing and quick response. Without this technology, the ability of Mauritian SMEs to compete in international markets is severely limited.

The results of our quantitative survey and our physical observations of the use of technology in the garment manufacturers we visited, would suggest that the SME textile sector is even less competitive.

Investment in plant and equipment – Of seven textile companies that quantified the change in value of their plant and equipment over the last twelve months, five had made no investment at all, one had increased value by 15% and another by 18%. Responding to the question of how significant a problem is the age of their machinery, three enterprises say it is a highly significant problem. Four out of eight firms state that age is not significant at all, yet these are the same companies that have not increased their investment in plant and equipment during the last twelve months. It may be that some of these firms have simply replaced old equipment without increasing the value of their investments, or some may have made substantial investment more than twelve months previously. Overall, it can be concluded that investment by SMEs in upgrading equipment is lower than required by the industry sector. A 1996 report into the technological competence of SMEs in Mauritius,[1] found that as much as 20% of SMEs had made no investment in new equipment or upgrading of current equipment within the last five years.

Maintenance – Field observations of eight garment manufacturers show that the majority are producing simple, low value-add products using relatively unsophisticated, standardised machines. These machines have a long working life, are easy to maintain and spare parts are readily available. This would explain the insignificance of machine age, and the responses to questions about the difficulty in getting spare parts and in maintaining equipment. Three out of nine companies say that getting spare parts was no problem and only one says that it is a highly significant problem. Maintaining equipment is hardly a problem for four out of nine companies, whilst for three it is moderately significant, and for only one it is a highly significant problem.

Only two companies are producing technically difficult products which require more sophisticated machinery: in one case, swimwear and in the other, lingerie. Neither company reported problems with the age or maintenance of their equipment. Rather, their major difficulties were the acquisition and retention of appropriate skills.

CAD/CAM systems – In our observations, one company producing printed T-shirts

---

[1] Dubois et al., (1996)

was using CAD to generate designs. Another company uses a computerised system for pattern generation and cutting. None use a fully integrated CAD/CAM system.

Computerised sewing/stitching – Virtually all firms use basic sewing machines.

Automated cloth-handling systems – Only one company has a semi-automated handling system. The rest are still using the traditional "bundle" system. This supports the findings of Lall and Wignaraja (1998).

Automation of post-CMT processes – Pressing, folding and packaging of finished garments is conducted manually throughout.

Group work systems – All firms, except one, use the assembly line system.

Effective quality control – Although all enterprises surveyed claim that they have quality control systems in place, only one has any type of formal system or documentation. This same company is the only one that is working towards ISO 9000. Quality control in the other organisations is achieved through informal visual checking by supervisors.

Management information and production control systems – There is little evidence of management information systems to monitor cost, inventory and production. It is likely that most SMEs do not know the exact profitability of their various product lines, do not understand issues relating to inventory and have no mechanisms for production planning.

Use of technical consultants – Of nine companies asked how often they used foreign technical consultants in the last five years, five had used no consultants at all, one had used consultants once, another four times, one company ten to twelve, and another stated that it had used consultants "a lot". Technical consultants are used primarily to solve production problems.

It is apparent that, in the majority of cases, SMEs in the garment manufacturing sector are using outdated, inefficient and ineffective technology, both in terms of equipment and processes.

3.2.3.2 Printing and Publishing

Printing and publishing in the developed world has undergone major changes over the last twenty years. The printing industry has segmented by product, e.g. newspapers, books, brochures, and has concentrated at the top-end owing to the increasing requirement for expensive capital equipment. Most traditional high-street printers serving local communities have turned themselves into copy shops.

The repro house, operating as the intermediate stage between design and print, has been absorbed and virtually eliminated by printers who have developed pre-press capabilities at all levels. Computerisation has been instrumental in integrating the different stages of the process, so that a design house or publisher can now output on-line and transmit directly by EDI (Electronic Data Interchange) to a printer who carries out the pre-press, print and post-press activities.

The main sources of international competitive advantage in the printing and publishing sector are:

- Seamless vertical process integration and rapid data transmission.
- High quality/low price proposition with the ability to produce in very high volumes.
- Guaranteed, fast delivery dates.

All of these sources of advantage depend on the effective use of state-of-the-art technology. Of the three industry sectors studied, capital intensity to achieve competitive advantage is highest in the printing and publishing sector, especially in traditional printing. Quality is directly related to the degree of technical sophistication of the capital equipment, the availability of appropriate skills, and effective production management and control.

A consultancy report on the Mauritian printing industry[2] explored the state of the industry in detail. Four of the companies we researched were also studied in this report. Of the remaining five printing companies we studied, we interviewed four that fall into the category of very small, domestic operations.

Our findings totally support those of the 1998 Commonwealth Secretariat report. In terms of technology capabilities, we too found that:

- Printing machinery is outdated
- Quality control is often poor. However, one company in our survey is already ISO 9000 registered, one is due to complete by the year 2000, and one is in the process of preparation.
- Pre-press capabilities exist and are generally adequate.

Use of technical consultants – In addition, we asked our sample how often they had used foreign technical consultants in the last five years. Of eight respondents, five do not used any at all. One firm used a consultant once, another three times, yet another used them "several" times.

3.2.3.3 IT

Despite the IT sector operating within a high technology environment, in most cases the actual technology used is relatively low-cost and readily available. The notable exception in our sample is the call centre that processes gambling bets from the US. Even here, the value of equipment is less than 1% of turnover.

The overarching problem facing IT companies is the cost of telecommunications, particularly for those transmitting data electronically overseas, and for all companies, there is a lack of appropriate skills.

---

[2] Commonwealth Secretariat (1998)

3.2.4 Human Resource Management

The strategic and operational importance of human resource management is now recognised worldwide. Techniques and practices to promote work motivation and productivity, organisational development and change strategies have enabled organisations to maximise employee effectiveness and to deliver competitive advantage in both domestic and international markets.

SMEs all over the world lag behind in these developments. This is partly a function of the particular structures and cultures of small businesses as they are determined by the nature of the owner-manager or entrepreneurial role. We shall discuss this later in the chapter. Additionally, the constant lack of resources often works against the adoption of progressive human resource policies, which are perceived to be expensive and time-consuming.

Within the time-scale of this study we could not assess HR approaches in any depth. Nor are we qualified to ascertain the impact of ethnic hierarchies and cultural responses on the management of people at work. Therefore we have, adopted some simple measures of human resource management. These include investment in training as an indication of management's commitment to its workforce; the degree of absenteeism and levels of staff turnover as measures of employee commitment; wage rates and output per worker to measure productivity; and the education of employees as a measure of level of skills. We have also included a short section on our impressions gained during our visits as to the "feel" of the culture of the company.

3.2.4.1 Investment in Training

Data on sixteen companies was available. The results are shown in the table below.

Table 3.8: Investment in Training as a Percentage of Turnover

Spend on training as % of turnover	Textiles	Printing and publishing	IT	Total
0%	3	5	0	8
<1%	3	1	1	5
>1% – <2%	1	0	1	2
>2%	1	0	0	1
Total	8	6	2	16

Although the sample is small, particularly in the printing and publishing and IT sectors, it is interesting that these two industries are the least willing to spend money on training despite their a major problem being a lack of available skills.

When asked how difficult it is to find the appropriate employee skills, where 1 is the least problem and 5 is the biggest, the following responses were given by 23 companies.

Table 3.9: Significance of the Problem of Finding Appropriate Employee Skills

Significance of problem	Textiles	Printing and publishing	IT	Total
1	0	0	0	0
2	2	2	1	5
3	3	2	0	5
4	2	1	1	4
5	4	3	2	9
Total	11	8	4	23

Overall, investment in training is pitifully low.

3.2.4.2 Absenteeism and Staff Turnover

Absenteeism is claimed to be a major problem throughout industry in Mauritius.

In our survey, 24 companies responded to the question: "How significant a problem is absenteeism in your business?", where 1 is least significant and 5 is most significant. The results are shown below.

Figure 3.3: Significance of Problem of Absenteeism

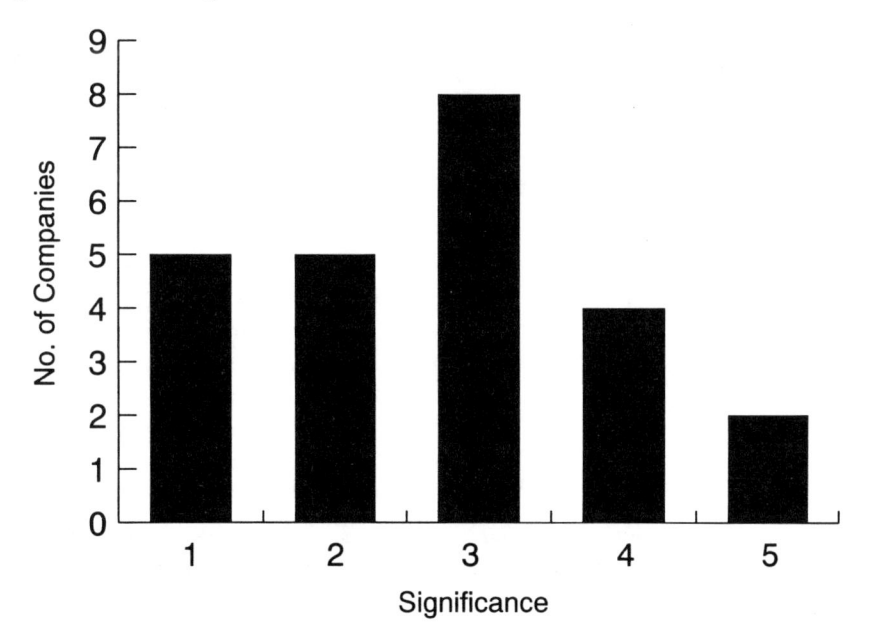

Of the five companies that rated absenteeism as least significant, one is an IT company and, another, one of the high-tech printing companies, both with professional management in place; one is a garment manufacture enterprise operating highly progressive management

practices, and two are in printing. Given its more difficult working conditions, it is not surprising that the textile industry finds absenteeism more of a problem.

It is surprising that only two companies ranked absenteeism as highly significant, despite the widespread awarding of attendance bonuses. Admitting a high level of absenteeism may be perceived by the responding manager as a sign of weakness or failure.

However, it should be recognised that absenteeism may be partly a function of the cultural characteristic of Mauritius, which could be categorised as "high collectivism", a term coined by Geert Hofstede in his seminal work on the impact of culture on organisational behaviour[3]. Here, the group takes precedence over the individual. Work is less a means of achieving individual job satisfaction and more a means to maintain family. This perspective has major implications for the commitment of employees to their jobs and their performance of task roles. Employees, particularly women, work hard for their families over the weekend. It is perhaps better to do more for the family and take Monday off to recover, than to put more effort into the job.

Staff turnover poses a significant problem in SMEs within the textile industry. In our discussions with interviewees, respondents complained that employees leave to work for larger companies as soon as there are vacancies, or shortly after receiving training. Wages and working conditions in larger companies are generally better than in the smaller enterprise. These findings are supported by Lall and Wignaraja (1998) report and our study too confirms that high staff turnover is a major disincentive for SMEs to invest in staff training.

Staff turnover appears to be significantly less of a problem in the other two industries we studied.

3.2.4.3 *Wage Rates and Employee Education*

As expected wage rates are heavily dependent on the industry sector, with textiles offering the lowest average rates to unskilled workers. Graduates appear to have the best opportunity to maximise their income within the IT industry.

The figures in the table below should be treated with some caution. The wide variation in wage rates for skilled workers, technicians and engineers could mean that respondents place technicians or engineers in the category of skilled workers

Table 3.10: Average Monthly Wage in Mauritian Rupees

	Unskilled workers	Skilled workers	Technicians	Engineers	Other graduates
Textiles	1,500 – 3,800	3,500 – 15,000	7,000 – 15,000	5,000 – 25,000	16,000
Printing /publishing	2,000 – 6,000	3,000 – 15,000	6,000 – 24,500	10,000	12,000 – 18,000
IT	3,700	4,500 – 8,000	7,200 – 20,000	10,800 – 25,000	

[3] Hofstede (1980)

Of seven garment manufacturing companies providing quantifiable data on wage rates, only three companies employed staff above the category of skilled workers, and only one employed staff in the "other graduate" category. SMEs surveyed in the other two industries employed several staff as technicians or engineers, and as could be expected, graduates were employed most intensely in the IT industry.

3.2.4.4 Impressions of Organisational Culture

The culture of an organisation is a major determinant of employees' performance. An individual's experience of their working conditions, the friendliness of colleagues and management, the general "feel" of the place can serve either to motivate or demotivate. We have not carried out a comprehensive analysis of organisational culture in the firms we visited, nevertheless, our first impressions can be useful.

Textiles – One firm implements policies that would be highly progressive in any cultural context. Garment makers are organised into teams, with each choosing a team leader. Group bonuses are given for meeting or exceeding production targets. There is a "Workers' Council" meeting every three months. Absenteeism is dealt with in an innovative manner. "Red Periods" are times when everybody is expected to exert an all-out effort and individuals are penalised if absent without a good reason. During "Green Periods", a reasonable level of absenteeism is tolerated. The owner-manager described how she copes with extended absenteeism associated with weddings: "On wedding days I expect everybody to work in the morning. Then, in the afternoon, we all go to the wedding, including me." This enterprise is situated in the middle of a small village and makes a major contribution to village life – to the school, and towards buildings and transport.

In contrast, we visited another factory, also situated in a very small town. On entering, we were affected by fumes. Several workers were printing T-shirts without any extraction, even though extractors were installed, and the air throughout the building was thick with fumes. When we asked about this, we were told that sometimes they turn on the extractors, but not today. In this same factory, women garment makers were hemmed into such a small space that they could not turn around or move their chairs. If they needed to go to the toilet, they would have to ask the person in the next row to get up.

These two examples demonstrate extremes of organisational culture and approaches to human resource management. Productivity per employee in both these firms is lower than average for the companies we surveyed, but the former employs more people, and has a much higher level of exports and cites absenteeism as a negligible problem. It is generally a more successful company.

Printing and publishing – We were shown around a number of printing works. In one, we sensed a paternalistic culture, with the owner-manager presenting himself as a "guardian" of his workers. Whether his employees agree with this we cannot tell without talking to them. We were also taken around one of the pre-press houses. The building is new and large, with much of the space still unoccupied. Staff were working on the latest computers in pleasant surroundings. The overall air was one of professionalism.

IT – As we were not shown around any of these companies, we cannot assess this culture.

3.2.5 Conclusions

Table 3.11 summarises our findings on the competences of the SME sector in Mauritius by the industry sectors examined.

3.11: Summary of competences

	Textiles
Marketing	
• Product	Product quality generally low Products lack differentiation Ranges too broad Limited use of branding
• Price	No use made of strategic pricing
• Promotion	Very low spend on promotion Overemphasis on personal selling Virtually no use made of direct marketing
• Distribution	Few arrangements with agents or distributors Underdevelopment of marketing channels
Design	Generally, design under-utilised Designers not integrated into business processes Lack of skills in setting design briefs and managing design projects
Technology	Outdated production technologies Weak in production management and materials handling Few management information systems Little use of technical consultants
Human resource	Investment in training low Major lack of employee skills Absenteeism a significant problem Staff turnover very high Low wage rates Low levels of employee education Culture sometimes repressive

3.2.5.1 Marketing

Our general impression of the marketing capabilities of the SMEs we researched is that very few of them have clear ideas of the role of marketing in their business. Little evidence was found of companies having a clear marketing strategy. Exceptions were in some of the more high-tech businesses, or in those whose activities and focus are dictated by a parent company. Since marketing strategy determines the nature of the marketing mix, we conclude that decisions on product, price, promotion or distribution

Printing and publishing	IT
Jobbing printers: quality generally low; non-specialised Specialists: quality moderate to high Pre-press: high quality, clearly defined proposition	Products and services offered too diverse to comment on product or service range, quality, etc
Heavy price competition where value-add is low	No information on pricing
Low spend on promotion Limited use of the total range of promotional tools	More varied use of promotional tools, particularly electronic media
Limited use of marketing intermediaries	More varied use of marketing channels
Limited use of design resource	
Antiquated machinery, particularly in the smaller companies Quality control generally poor Pre-press capabilities adequate Little use of technical consultants	Level of technology consistent with business objectives
Investment in training low Major lack of employee skills Absenteeism a moderate problem Staff turnover moderate Moderate wage rates Low levels of employee education	Investment in training very low Major lack of employee skills Absenteeism manageable Staff turnover is not a problem Attractive wage rates Moderate levels of education

are generally made on an ad hoc basis. Without a competitive marketing strategy, it is unlikely that these decisions will be effective.

As will be seen in Chapter 5, institutional support for SMEs in the area of marketing concentrates on the tools of the marketing mix, with very little attention given to help develop a successful marketing strategy.

3.2.5.2 Design

Design effectiveness is extremely difficult to assess, particularly quantitatively. The absolute measure of how many and what type of designers are used is insufficient. Many designers may be used simply to ensure that a garment or printing material is productionable. Our observations reveal little evidence of the extra flair, originality or excitement of good design that makes the difference between a product that is competitive and successful in export markets and one that is mundane.

Designers need a very rich and varied environment from which to draw ideas and inspiration. In Mauritius we suspect that many of them, no matter how well trained, have limited or ineffective exposure to these sources. In addition, design can only be as good as the design brief given, and we also suspect that very few managers of SMEs have experience of managing either designers or the design process.

The enhancement of a design culture in Mauritius is feasible and in Chapter 6 we propose an initiative that could help to propagate good design and design management.

3.2.5.3 Technology

The technology needs of the three sectors varies considerably. In textiles, the acquisition and maintenance of the machinery itself is less significant a factor in achieving competitive advantage than the technologies related to production management and materials handling. Much more help needs to be given to SMEs in acquiring these skills.

For very small enterprises in the printing and publishing industry, the cost of acquiring modern printing machines may not be justified by the volumes and value of work available. Instead, as the Pira report suggests, they should be investigating the opportunities presented by new low-cost electronic technologies in the area of pre-press, pre-media and communications services. Those serving the domestic market might consider reinventing themselves as copy shops, along the lines of Kall Kwik and Prontaprint in the UK (see Box 3.1).

But many SMEs are ill-equipped to make these are strategic decisions. For institutional support to focussing on "technology", without a recognition of strategy, fails to provide appropriate assistance.

Box 3.1: Bringing printing to the high street – The case of Kall Kwik

The advent of new technology has changed the face of small-scale printing in the UK. At one time, every High Street had a small printer servicing local businesses and individuals with corporate and personal stationery. Now, they have completely disappeared, to be replaced by the drop-in copy shop. Two major franchised chains dominate this new industry – Kall Kwik and Prontaprint – both offering design, copy and print services. A typical Kall Kwik branch will have a number of photocopying machines ranging from very small coin-operated ones that customers can use themselves to large commercial machines that can replicate high quality black and white print, and which are economically viable at much smaller print runs than the traditional printing machine. Colour copying, the production of transparencies for overhead projectors, laminating and binding, enlarging and reducing are additional over-the-counter services offered. Both chains offer customised graphic design services, as well as traditional two-colour printing; they sell standardised social or greeting cards that can be overprinted, and a range of stationery products.

Turnaround is very fast, from immediate service on an as-you-wait basis to only a few days for customised printing. Customers can download data directly via email to the Kall Kwik branch for collection later that day.

Kall Kwik and Prontaprint have made design and printing services fast, accessible and affordable for the individual or the smaller business, leaving the traditional printers to concentrate on higher quality, higher volume and more complex work for large corporate customers.

3.2.5.4 Human Resource

Overall, the textile sector demonstrates poor use of human resources. Low levels of employee skills are compounded by minimal investment in training. De-motivated employees tend towards absenteeism, high staff turnover and low productivity. The printing and publishing industry appears to make better use of people, whilst the IT sector attracts and rewards the most able personnel.

Like SMEs all over the world, those in Mauritius have difficulty in implementing effective human resource management strategies and practices. This problem is compunded by the Anglo-American origins of the theory on which "good" practice is based – it takes no account of the cultural differences of non-Western societies.[4] In contrast the progressive textile company mentioned earlier has taken these theories and adapted them to its specific circumstances. SME support institutions in Mauritius

[4] Mendonca and Kanungo (1996)

might consider conducting a research project to identify appropriate human resource management techniques and practices that could result in an extensive training programme for owner-managers of SMEs.

3.3 Strategy

For a small or medium enterprise to be successful internationally it needs a clearly defined strategy for both entering and maintaining a viable position in selected markets. The two key tasks in developing such a strategy are:

- identifying and selecting a target market
- creating and implementing a competitive advantage.

We shall explore these and consider whether and how the firms in our sample make strategic choices.

3.3.1 Market Selection

Market selection follows these stages:

Gathering information on markets – Market knowledge is gained in two ways: desk research, e,g. reading country and market reports, statistical data, finding out about competitors; and through primary research, e.g. talking to customers, distributors, agents, and by personal visits to potential markets.

Three problems face the typical SME in carrying out desk research on potential export markets. Firstly, they may have little understanding of what to look for. Currently, the role and process of business research is usually only taught on management courses. Only one chief executive in our sample has an MBA and two hold first degrees in management. Of the others, qualified to first degree level, most have studied technical subjects related to their type of activity. The second problem derives from the sheer scale of available information. This makes it difficult for the owner-manager to sift through and pull out the relevant parts. Lastly, the everyday pressures on heads of SMEs and their lack of time and resources prevents them standing back and adopting a strategic, longer-term perspective.

In our research, we asked respondents about their use of information sources, specifically SMIDO's Documentation Centre, the information services offered by EPZDA, and MEDIA's Trade Information Centre. The results are shown in detail in Chapter 5. We also aimed to assess the degree of primary research undertaken by our sample in terms of personal contact with overseas markets through attending buyer/seller meets or trade fairs. Our findings support our estimation that very few SMEs are actually using the information services available locally.

Conducting primary research is probably even more difficult for the average SME and particularly so in Mauritius given its geographical isolation and the relative cost of travel to income. It is, therefore, disappointing to see that the majority of SMEs in our sample have not used the opportunities offered by MEDIA in its buyer/seller meets or trade fairs. These findings are consistent with those of De Chazal Du Mee (1998). Possible reasons for this will also be discussed in Chapter 5.

It is clear that SMEs, by themselves, have great difficulty in even beginning the process of developing successful export strategies. As a first stage, much more *direct* help is needed by SMEs to identify the countries and market segments that hold most promise.

Evaluating markets and assessing strategic fit – Markets are evaluated on factors such as size, growth, concentration, cost structures, ease of entry, competitive offerings, and customer needs. For an SME to assess its chances of successfully entry to a given market, it needs to understand what proposition would deliver competitive advantage in that market, whether it already has the capabilities to deliver such a proposition, and if not, what it would need to do to enhance its capabilities. Such an evaluation has major financial implications. The firm must understand the various concepts of cost, breakeven, and the relationship between cost, volume and profit. It needs an understanding of different pricing strategies and how they impact on profitability; of the importance of cash flow; of investment appraisal and the time value of money; and of different ways of assessing return on investment.

The recent report on the printing industry, mentioned earlier, concludes that overall financial management within the sector is poor, particularly with regard to knowledge of costs. The decision to adopt a low-cost or added value proposition, for example, is critically dependent on cost structures both within the market generally and the SME in particular. A lack of proper management accounting procedures will be a major inhibitor to exporting.

Financial accounting seems to be better understood and used. Of sixteen enterprises that responded to a question on how often they forecast and updated cashflows, two never used them at all, but six updated and forecast on a monthly basis. Again, SMEs need more hands-on assistance in evaluating markets and assessing their own capabilities. This requires high-level managerial skills and it is unreasonable to assume that SMEs achieve this themselves. These two stages concerned with market selection form the first part of developing an export strategy.

3.3.2 Competitive Advantage

The principal sources of competitive advantage for SMEs wishing to export are widely cited as:

- offering meaningful differentiation in a limited number of relatively small markets ("nicheing")
- developing good relations with overseas distributors and agents[5]

[5] Katsikeas et al (1997), Yeoh et al (1995), Wren et al (1998), Simpson and Paul (1995)

These link to the next two stages of the export initiation process.

Developing a proposition – If a market appears promising and the firm has, or can develop, sufficient capabilities to serve that market, then they can decide the best positioning within that market. The two basic positionings are to offer value through lower-cost and, therefore, a lower price to the consumer; or to offer value through differentiation and/or customisation. The literature of SMEs[6] indicates that a niche strategy, offering differentiation, customisation or innovation, is the most achievable and maintainable position.

The textile companies we visited were asked whether they are pursuing a low-cost or high quality strategy. All said they were aiming at a high quality strategy, yet from our observations only two offered a significant degree of differentiation, customisation or innovation in their products. The rest were producing "me-too" products that would lack competitiveness in most overseas markets.

Interestingly, the two firms delivering differentiation both had CEOs who had either lived abroad or who have ongoing personal experience of overseas markets. "Differentness" is relative and it is impossible to know how to be different and interesting if one has a limited perspective. We will link this later to the discussion on the type of mindset needed to export successfully, but it indicates that, for many SMEs in Mauritius, the limitations of a small remote island can be a major handicap to innovation.

Market entry – Having developed a differentiated proposition, the potential exporter should consider how to enter the selected market. For most SMEs, the most effective method is to develop relationships with distributors or agents. Although, in our assessment of distribution capabilities, some of the firms we surveyed are using agents or wholesalers, our overall impression is that in most cases these relationships tend to be ad hoc and opportunistic.

The challenge for the SME sector is to develop more formal, enduring and favourable relationships with distributors. This requires knowledge and time, and is therefore difficult for the individual entrepreneur to achieve. We are proposing, in our last chapter, a framework for helping SMEs enter new markets more easily.

The small scale and capacity of most SMEs is a significant barrier to exporting. One of our respondents in the garment manufacturing business had to refuse an order from an overseas buyer because he was unable to supply in sufficient volume. Establishing consortia of SMEs in a particular industry sector, where members collaborate in developing differentiated, distinctive propositions, and perhaps centralise functions such as design and materials sourcing, might overcome this problem. We will discuss this later in more depth.

Subcontracting is another well-tried mechanism for small companies to enter overseas markets. No one in our sample is involved in any form of subcontracting. All are trying to "go it alone". Although Mauritius has a framework for linking companies through subcontracting (SUBEX), this only applies to firms engaged in engineering activities.

---

[6] For example, Barber et al (ed . 1992); Porter (1980); Hall (1995)

Competitive advantage through new technologies – Recent developments in telecommunications have opened up new international business possibilities for many SMEs. Many of the disadvantages of size, scale and location of the small firm have been neutralised and they are better able to investigate, make contact with, and enter new markets. For example, shopping via the internet and digital television is likely to create the biggest retail revolution for a century, and one in which SMEs are as likely to succeed as their biggest competitors. In the companies we visited, only a few use the internet regularly or even have email facilities. Some of them have no computers at all.

The diffusion of computer technology at the simplest and lowest level should be a major priority of Mauritius. Britain recognised this some time ago in the 1980s when it gave computers to every school in the country. Liberalisation and privatisation in the telecommunications sector in Mauritius should be expedited to ensure low-cost communications. This would encourage the establishment of new forms of enterprise, such as internet cafés, CD Rom authoring, offshore data entry and software development.

3.3.3 Conclusions

Many SMEs in Mauritius appear to have set up in business in order to produce what they can or what they are good at, but then wait for customers. Few seem to have developed a clear export strategy based on analysis of sound information. In our questionnaire, we asked respondents to identify their growth strategy for the next five years in terms of Ansoff's matrix of marketing objectives: market penetration, product development, market development and diversification. It should be noted that this question was phrased in non-jargon language.

One small company feels that their market development strategy is to "look for new customers and bigger orders" and their diversification strategy is to "reduce cost of production by buying new machines". Clearly, this owner-manager has little idea of what constitutes strategy. Some of our respondents fully understood the question and answered with seemingly clearly thought out and feasible strategies. However, these are mainly the larger, well-established companies among the sample.

The three-year business plan is the principle framework for formulating strategy. All SMEs should be encouraged to undertake business planning on a regular basis. One method is to insist on the submission of a strategic business plan before any financial loans or grants can be made. Since SMEs in Mauritius have access to many forms of financial assistance – bank loans at preferential rates, training subsidies, etc – this is a relatively easy mechanism.

It is unrealistic to assume that the smaller enterprises are able by themselves to develop appropriate growth and export strategies. In our view they need much more direct help and hand-holding. Some of our proposals in the last chapter address this need.

3.4 Managerial Characteristics

For SMEs in Mauritius exporting is the principal growth strategy. Substantial research has been undertaken into growth in small firms and the discourse generally falls under three headings: market opportunities and structure; resources, specifically access to finance, skilled labour and technology; and management and motivation. Whilst the firm's operating environment is outside of its control, a successful growth strategy capitalises on external opportunities and implements appropriate and timely changes in the firm's internal organisation. This process is dependent on the growth orientation of the owner-manager, which is predominantly driven by his or her managerial characteristics.

The three managerial characteristics we are considering in relation to Mauritian SMEs are:

- the commitment of the owner-manager to growth, and thereby to exporting, and the managerial skills that foster growth

- the export orientation of the owner-manager in terms of perception of risk and willingness to commit resources

- the mindset of the owner-manager in terms of a global or international perspective.

3.4.1 Commitment to Growth

It cannot be assumed that all small businesses are interested in growth. Three categories of small business can be identified. Those that are created for the specific purpose of income substitution (the mom and pop shop) will be satisfied with just sufficient turnover to generate a basic living for family members. These tend to remain as micro-enterprises. The second category encompasses those businesses whose owner-manager aims for a standard of living significantly higher than would be achievable through employment. Typically, this sort of firm will grow sufficiently to offer employment to, perhaps, tens of people, but is unlikely to step out of the SME category. The third type of business has an inherent growth orientation and, unless prevented by negative environmental conditions, demonstrates rapid, quantitative growth from the outset.

Of the SMEs surveyed, only one company achieved more than 40% growth, in this case 56%. Although the number of respondents is far too small to give a representative view, the growth rates are disappointing. Of these thirteen companies, seven were established in the 1990s, five in the 1980s and one in 1974. Only three are less than five years old and of those three, one achieved growth of 0.2%, another 35% and the other 40%. It should also be noted that the company showing 35% growth is, in number of employees, larger than the definition of an SME. If we assume that a growth-oriented company achieves rapid growth in its formative years, then only one out of the thirteen would appear to fall into the third category of business. Even then, a new fast growing company could expect to at least double its turnover annually.[7]

In the literature, correlations have been found between personality characteristics and growth-orientation of the small business owner-manager. It may be of interest to public sector or other SME support institutions to have a way of identifying growth-orientation in order to maximise the effectiveness of investment in building or enhancing entrepreneurial skills. A "Growth Club" targeted at the owner-managers of small businesses with growth potential has been tried in Durham, UK.

For a company to grow, it must acquire a broader range of skills, competences and perspectives than the owner-manager alone can supply. It needs to empower others working in the organisation and create an organisational structure that can cope with complexity. Since a major motive for small business start-ups is the owner-manager's desire for control, he or she may resist the necessary move towards management delegation.

Of the SMEs interviewed, only six are not managed on a day-to-day basis by the owner. Of these six, four are wholly- or majority-owned by non-Mauritians; three are within the IT sector, two are the French-owned pre-press service facilities, and only one is in textiles. Given the low level of managerial skills of many owner-managers, SMEs in Mauritius may continue to remain small and, in terms of this study, continue to struggle with exporting.

Enhancing managerial skills through the traditional routes of academic learning, or even short courses and workshops, in our view is largely ineffective and certainly inappropriate for the busy owner-manager of an SME. These courses are de-contextualised, ill-suited to the hands-on approach of the entrepreneur, and consume too many resources. On-the-job training is significantly more appropriate and we propose, in the last chapter, systems of mentoring and shadowing that could enhance managerial skills quickly and effectively.

3.4.2 Export Orientation

A research study,[8] into the export propensity of very small food and beverage processing firms in Australia, identified the export orientation of the owner-manager as one of the most important influences on export potential. The research concluded that successful exporting companies had owner-managers who were totally committed to exporting and who were prepared to commit substantial resources.

Our impressions of the companies we visited are that only two or three of them are sufficiently committed to developing export business to make it a priority. It is possible that the issues related to lack of export skills are so inhibiting that owner-managers feel overwhelmed. Supporting institutions in Mauritius could consider facilitating the establishment of dedicated, sector- or market-specific export houses that could take

---

[7] Firm growth is a function of many factors including the size of the firm, the structure-conduct-performance characteristics of its industry, the nature of its ownership, its skill base, and so on. It is recognised that managerial commitment is only one influence, albeit a particularly important one.
[8] Philp (1998)

on many of these exporting functions. This idea will be discussed in more detail in the last chapter.

Another study, this time of SMEs in New Zealand,[9] identified that owner-managers' perceptions of the risks involved and the profit potential in exporting were instrumental in whether they adopted a strategic intent to export. The assessment of risks and future profits is made relative to the domestic market. Although initial exporting activity delivered less profit than from domestic markets, the longitudinal study found a perception that exporting would deliver future profits was steadfastly maintained by the companies that became the most successful exporters. In addition, the study found that new exporters were most comfortable exporting to markets with the closest "psychic distance", in this case, Australia and the Pacific Islands. Once experience was gained in these markets, firms were more likely to attempt exporting farther afield.

These insights should help SME support organisations to develop initiatives that firstly, reduce the actual risk of exporting. Several ideas have already been put forward and will be explored in more detail in Chapter 6 of this study. Secondly, the support sector may consider ways to enhance and maintain perceptions of export profitability through, perhaps, widely publicising and rewarding profitable export achievements. Lastly, if exporting initially to the Indian Ocean islands sits within an owner-manager's "comfort zone", then perhaps more could be done on a collaborative basis to target those markets more effectively.

3.4.3 A Global or International Mindset

In our view, exposure to international influences is a significant factor in developing differentiated propositions. We contend that where the owner-manager has had extensive contact with other societies, he or she is better able to develop a successful exporting business. Of the companies we observed those with the highest level of exports, owner-managers had lived abroad, studied in Europe or the US, or, in one case, travelled extensively.

This is supported by a study of global mindsets and their influence on Third World businesses.[10] A global mindset is not just about knowledge of the world. It is a set of attitudes and beliefs that encompasses elements such as curiosity; the acceptance of complexity, diversity and uncertainty; trust in others and the ability to delegate; a focus on continuous improvement; and a long-term view. Mauritius' small size, together with its geographical and cultural limitations, make it difficult for people who have rarely left the island to develop this mindset. It is impossible to change people overnight, but infusing a more outward-looking approach is feasible. There are many ways to do this and we will discuss some of them in the final chapter.

---

[9] Chetty and Hamilton
[10] Srinivas (1995)

3.4.4 Conclusions

Traditionally, enterprise policy has focused on two main concerns: increasing the net birth rate of firms and creating a favourable external environment. Increasingly, attention is being focused on the endogenous drivers of growth, the "soft" values, the less tangible and less quantitative factors that determine the high-growth small firm. If we accept that the owner-manager of an SME is the single most important determinant of how successful the firm becomes, then his or her personal characteristics assume a much greater role.

It is improbable that entrepreneurship can be taught. It depends on a set of values, attitudes and beliefs involving perceptions of risk, self-concept, creativity and fun. However, it is possible to identify and target potential entrepreneurs (and perhaps develop an entrepreneurial "hothouse") to help them fulfil their potential. Basic managerial skills and capabilities, however, can be developed in most people who are interested in business, and higher level managerial skills can be nurtured in many ways.

In the next century a culture of innovation will be critical to the success of nations. Mauritius must create for new and successive generations the mindset that will give it the national comparative advantage of innovation.

4 Policy and Procedural Regime for SMEs

4.1 Introduction

This chapter analyses the nature of macroeconomic, trade and industrial policies in Mauritius pertaining to the fostering of competitiveness in individual SMEs and SME clusters. For convenience, the relevant policy regime issues are considered under three broad headings: policy impediments, procedural impediments and infrastructure impediments. The first concerns incentive policies that affect the relative attractiveness of domestic market production and exporting, the second concerns bureaucratic procedures/regulations that affect transaction costs involved in small enterprise start-up and operation, and the third affects small enterprise production costs and country reputation. The aim of the chapter is not to be exhaustive but to focus on those aspects of the policy regime, which in the Commonwealth mission's view, pose the biggest constraints to small firms.

4.2 Policies and Procedures: SME Views

In terms of its trade, industrial and macroeconomic regime; Mauritius is an outlier from other African developing economies. Unlike many African developing economies, the country did not subscribe to the prevailing orthodoxy of inward-oriented, state dominated development strategies of the 1960s and 1970s that emphasised stringent import substitution coupled with heavy state intervention in the economy. Instead in the 1970s, Mauritius followed a mixed trade policy of import substitution coupled with incentives for exports through the Export Processing Zone (EPZ).[1] These two trade regimes co-existed, influencing enterprises producing for the small home market and those producing for export. Furthermore to its credit, Mauritius began trade liberalisation in 1983 as a part of its 1981 structural adjustment loan agreement with the World Bank.

Three distinct phases of trade liberalisation and industrial reforms can be identified since the mid-1980s, each with a different rate of reform and coverage.

- The first episode, between 1983-85, consisted of the rapid elimination of most quantitative restrictions on imports and their replacement by tariffs. Existing incentives for exporting – granted via the EPZ since 1970 – were maintained. Repeated attempts were made to attract export-oriented foreign investment. Moreover, macroeconomic stability in the form of low inflation

[1] Woldekidan (1994), Milner and McKay (1996) and Lall and Wignaraja (1998).

and competitive interest and exchange rates became an explicit policy objective. Despite these early market-oriented reforms, the domestic manufacturing sector remained relatively highly protected and the private sector was restricted by a plethora of bureaucratic regulations.

- The second, between 1986-1993, tried to gradually reduce the dispersion of effective protection among industries and to promote exports more vigorously by providing exporters with overseas marketing support, preferential interest rates on development loans and tax concessions. Export and foreign investment promotion was greatly strengthened by the creation of a specialised agency, the Mauritius Export Development and Investment Authority (MEDIA) in 1985. Emphasis was also placed on maintaining macroeconomic and price stability. There were also useful cuts in bureaucratic procedures and regulations affecting imports, exports, foreign exchange allocations etc. The net result of these reforms was that the economy became more outward-oriented and private-sector focussed than in the past.

- The third episode, from 1994 to date, attempted to cut protection further by reducing import tariffs and attempting to develop new areas of comparative advantage. Although the government reduced the number of tariff bands and made a cut in maximum import tariff rates in 1995, no specific targets seem to have been set to achieve a low uniform rate of effective protection. The development of new exports was recognised as a pressing issue and new institutions were established to achieve this end. In particular, the Mauritius Productivity and Competitiveness Council was conceived in 1998 to provide strategic guidance in fostering new skill-intensive exports. Plans were drawn up for a separate Board of Investment to facilitate the entry of high skill inward investment as well to streamline approval procedures. Corporate taxation was reduced for EPZ firms.

The results from the survey of 34 randomly selected small and medium enterprises (SMEs) in the garments, printing and information technology (IT) sectors helps identify specific policy areas, which require immediate reform to accelerate SME competitiveness in Mauritius.[2] The firm-level interviews indicate that the trade and industrial reforms (implemented in 1986-1993 and accelerated from the mid-1990s onwards) have led to considerable improvements in the business environment for the private sector – including SMEs. The trade and industrial regime in Mauritius in 1998/1999 is much more liberal than in the past and is one of the most open and market-friendly in Africa. The country has emphasised export promotion policies and given incentives to expand exports. Many enterprises detect increasing sensitivity and responsiveness of the Government to the concerns of the small firm sector. These are creditable achievements

[2] These were surveyed through postal questionnaires and face-to-face interviews. Of these, about 25 enterprises provided quantitative data for this chapter. The enterprise survey is described in Appendix

even by the standards of many middle-income Asian developing economies.

Nevertheless, the SME survey showed that there are some important policy and procedural impediments, which hamper the growth and competitiveness of small firms in 1998/1999. The aggregate results for 25 small enterprises are shown in Figure 4.1. The sample firms scored the major obstacles on a scale of 1 to 5 according to their degree of negative impact on business. The enterprise scores on a particular variable were then summed-up and averaged for the whole sample. A score of 1 is regarded as the least negative impact and 5 as most negative impact.

The survey suggests that on average small firms believe that macroeconomic issues – high interest rates, high taxation/VAT level concerns and (to a lesser extent) exchange rates movements – are among the strongest obstacles to operating their business and moving into exports. Conversely, however, policy uncertainty (in the sense of unpredictable, and non-transparent implementation of government policies and rules that affect a small firm's daily business) does not generally rank as a major issue.

The concern with high interest rates is also closely related to an important financial sector problem for small firms: a lack of access to bank finance. Interestingly, our subsequent interviews with enterprises suggests there is little difference in the conservative approach of private commercial banks and the state-owned Development Bank of Mauritius (DBM) as suppliers of short-term working capital (or long-term investment finance) to small firms.

Following these macroeconomic and financial sector concerns, small firms report being badly impaired by some cumbersome bureaucratic regulations and procedures on business start-up and operation. In this regard, procedures affecting access to imported raw materials and equipment show up as a significant impediment (see Section 4.3.2.1). Other bureaucracy is also mentioned as a problem. Disaggregation of the survey data suggested that this concern is largely due to rules governing small business start-up (see Section 4.4.2). With the exception of a few persistent impediments, firms suggest that the degree of bureaucratic control of business activities has declined over time.

In the area of labour market impediments, the main concern arises from strict rules governing the hiring foreign workers and technicians. Other issues impairing labour market flexibility include the level of the minimum wage and stringent regulations on laying-off workers.

Apart from the principal concerns listed above, a few small firms also pointed to dumping of goods by EPZ firms on the local market, harassment by customs officials and the limited size of the local market.

It is interesting to note that some of our findings were echoed in a mid-1998 May survey of 55 SMEs commissioned by SMIDO and carried out by a local accounting firm. The SME survey by De Chazal Du Mee (1998) highlighted the bureaucratic problems experienced in small enterprise business start-up and operation, fears about the administrative burden of VAT introduction and the lack of duty exemption on equipment purchase and raw materials. However, the De Chazal Du Mee survey shed no light on impediments to small firms stemming from the lack of policy reform and macroeconomic stability or labour market impediments.

As in the case of all firm-level surveys, the results of our survey should not be regarded as definitive indicators of key issues of small enterprise development in Mauritius. Rather it provides evidence of how the business environment appears from the important but subjective perspective of the private sector. To obtain a wider perspective on these issues, the Commonwealth mission spoke to government officials, economists, representatives of financial institutions and business associations, and visited enterprises.

Fig 4.1: Policy Obstacles to SMEs

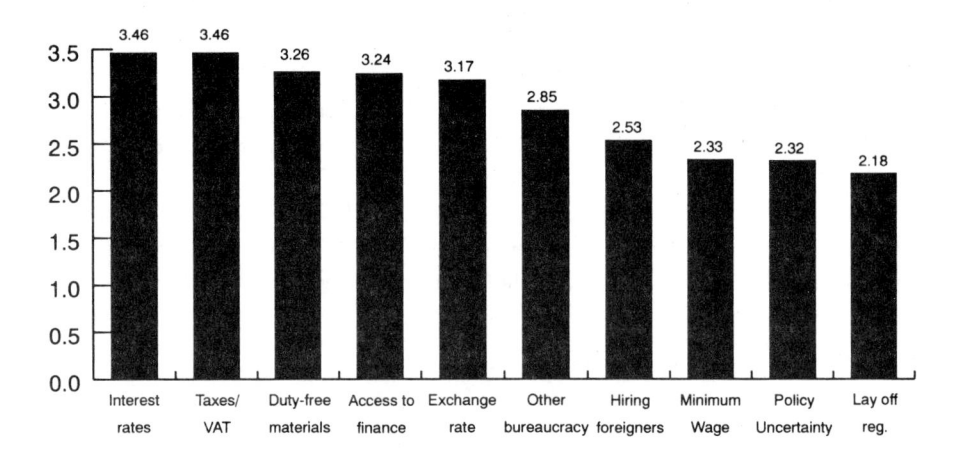

Category	Value
Interest rates	3.46
Taxes/VAT	3.46
Duty-free materials	3.26
Access to finance	3.24
Exchange rate	3.17
Other bureaucracy	2.85
Hiring foreigners	2.53
Minimum Wage	2.33
Policy Uncertainty	2.32
Lay off reg.	2.18

4.3 Selected Policy Impediments

4.3.1 Tariff Structure

As we have seen, Mauritius has been gradually moving from a mixed trade policy of import substitution coupled with incentives for exports through the Export Processing Zone (EPZ) in the 1970s to a more open, export-oriented economy in the 1980s and 1990s. Several episodes of import liberalisation have been attempted – last actions were in 1995 when the number of tariff bands were reduced and maximum import tariff rates were cut. By the mid-1990s, substantial progress was made in reducing tariffs and non-tariff barriers to imports in Mauritius. One indication of greater openness is that the average tariff for manufacturing fell from 86.2% in 1980 to 30.1% in 1994. [3]

The main changes include: quantitative restrictions have been mostly eliminated and the few that remain are largely on health, sanitary and security grounds; there are few

---

[3] WTO (1996); Lall and Wignaraja (1998)

import prohibitions (with the exception of commodities such as second hand motor vehicle spares and explosives); the level of nominal tariffs has fallen as well as its dispersion (the number of rate bands were cut from 60 to 8 and the maximum rates were reduced); there are no local content programmes to assist local suppliers; and public procurement policies are minimal. In July 1998, the country had an 8 band tariff system as follows: 0%, 5%, 15%, 20%, 30%, 40%, 55 & 75%, and 80 &100%. Despite this progress, the process of tariff reform seems to have faltered and remains far from complete in achieving the desirable goal of a low uniform rate of effective protection. Far more serious is that the Government seems not to have any plans for further tariff reductions.

At present, some industrial sectors are still quite highly protected by tariff barriers to trade while others are completely open. Table 4.1 provides the latest tariff rates for finished goods in selected manufacturing and service activities: software, information technology, printing and textiles receive no tariff protection; metal products and machinery receive medium-levels of protection; and clothing, food, footwear and furniture receive high levels of tariff protection. Chapter 2 (Table 2.4) illustrates the SME intensity of manufacturing establishments by industrial branch. Some sectors with a large population of SMEs (including food products, footwear and furniture) are very highly protected while the remainder receives negligible protection.

Table 4.1:   Tariffs on Finished Goods, July 1998

Item	Tariff Rate
Food products	55-80%
Textiles (fabrics)	Mostly 0%
Clothing	80%
Footwear	30% or 80%
Furniture	80%
Printing	0%
Metal Products (iron and steel)	20-55%
Machinery	15-40%
Information technology	0%
Software	0%

Source: Ministry of Finance Database, August 1998.

In general, international experience points to free trade as superior to protection because of better resource allocation according to comparative advantage; the realisation of economies of scale; access to new technologies, skills and markets; and the spur of competition to cut costs, improve productivity and achieve technical efficiency. Moderate protection is sometimes justified on "infant industry" grounds by the need for industrial latecomers to gain sufficient breathing space to learn to absorb new and complex technologies. However, the existing pattern of protection granted to particular activities in Mauritius does not seem to escalate according to skill and technology intensity (and hence learning costs and infant industry grounds).[4] Nor does it relate to increasing presence of small firms, which may have less industrial experience relative to large firms and multinationals. As such, there seems little economic rationale for the existing pattern of tariff protection. In addition, Mauritian membership of the WTO means that the country has signed up for sweeping import liberalisation in accordance with the Uruguay Round Agreements and a reduction in subsidy-based methods of export promotion. Thus, further liberalisation is the optimal policy option for SME growth and competitiveness.

4.3.2 EXPORT PROMOTION

In the short term, to cope with the situation of incomplete import liberalisation in the short-term and to reduce the anti-export bias of the trade regime, the Government of Mauritius provides some general measures to assist its exporters. The principal means of support which affect SMEs are:

- providing export-oriented firms with access to raw materials and equipment at world prices for export production;
- providing overseas marketing support for actual and potential SME exporters.

4.3.2.1. Access to Duty Free Imported Inputs

Under the scheme, EPZ firms can import a list of goods exempt from duties and sales taxes while non-EPZ firms are entitled to a duty drawback on the proportion of imported inputs used in making exports. The refunds to non-EPZ firms must be claimed from Customs within a six-month period of importing. This situation can pose impediments for sub-contractors and suppliers in general. The Government is aware of this situation and is attempting to alleviate some of the problems this has caused. Nevertheless, substantial problems remain. These can be illustrated by reference to three possible cases:

(1) *An EPZ textile and clothing firm is in a Cut, Making and Trimming (CMT) sub-contracting arrangement with an SME.* A practical route for the SME to gain duty-free access to imported inputs is by obtaining an EPZ certificate. Even in textiles and clothing where CMT arrangements are common, firm-level interviews suggested that approval for an EPZ certificate could take between 1-2 months from submission of the paperwork to the relevant administrative committee. Although approval times have improved significantly (down from 3-6 months previously), the delay and element of administrative discretion causes unnecessary business uncertainty for

---

[4] For instance, metal products, machinery and printing, usually regarded as medium to high skill activities, receive modest or no protection while simple activities – like food products, footwear and furniture – are very well protected.

SMEs and possible cancellation of orders. The firm-level interviews in industrial sectors with no CMT arrangements, further suggested that approval times may be longer than for textiles and EPZ certificates may be harder to obtain for SMEs. As the Mauritian industrial base grows and diversifies, this may pose a bottleneck to SME expansion.

(2) *An EPZ firm makes an ad hoc order to an SME and provides it with the raw materials duty-free.* The problem is wastage provision. Factory production usually involves an element of raw material wastage, which often cannot be accounted for. In order to ensure smooth functioning of duty-free raw material access, governments normally provide for a wastage ratio in a given order. Such wastage ratios are thought to exist for textiles and clothing but not for other industries. In turn, this can penalise ad hoc sub-contracting and cluster formation in new areas.

(3) *An EPZ firm makes an order to a non-EPZ SME.* Here the non-EPZ firm is entitled to a duty drawback on the proportion of imported inputs used in making exports. However, this process of re-claming duty drawback is subject to variable administrative delays. A recent study found that processing times could vary between 4-24 weeks in Mauritius in comparison with only 2 weeks in Sri Lanka and 2-6weeks in Indonesia.[5] This constraint discourages non-EPZ SMEs from the benefits of engaging in indirect exporting activities and forming clusters.

The analysis suggests that urgent action should be taken to reduce the transactions costs to small business in procedures affecting the duty-free access to imported inputs. This is one area where relatively painless reform can have immediate payoffs to SME growth. Streamlining, using paperless communications systems, and setting maximum processing times would form elements of a coherent solution. Raw material wastage provisions should also be extended to all potential export sectors to facilitate intermittent sub-contracting and intra-firm relations.

4.3.2.2 Overseas Marketing Support

In the past public policy did not seem to pay much attention to the overseas marketing needs of SMEs in Mauritius. However, this has changed since the mid-1990s. The Government has encouraged MEDIA and SMIDO to work more closely to identify and develop capable SMEs to become export-oriented. At present, a variety of MEDIA's overseas marketing services have been actively targeted to encourage SMEs to export (particularly to African markets such as Mozambique). The full range of MEDIA's services are available to SMEs including buyer-seller meets, contact promotion programmes, one-to-one meetings, industry-level market surveys and general and specific trade information. Some of these are provided free of charge to SMEs and others are part-subsidised. These services and enterprise viewpoints on them are

---

[5] Lall and Wignaraja (1998), p. 63.

examined in more detail in Chapter 5 (Section 5.5).

Most unfortunately, no aggregate data was available on the beneficiaries of MEDIA's services over time by firm size, industry membership and export history. During our interviews, MEDIA officials suggested that, historically the take-up rate of overseas marketing services among SMEs has been quite low. MEDIA estimates that only about 40-50 SMEs on SMIDO's list can meet the rigorous demands of overseas markets (in terms of price, quality and delivery deadlines) and even fewer have approached MEDIA for assistance during the last year. In our view, this may be owing to several inter-related reasons:

- MEDIA and SMIDO have not sufficiently publicised these services to potential SME exporters (and sought them out for tailor-made assistance);
- MEDIA has too many responsibilities (export promotion, investment promotion and managing industrial estates) and has insufficient time to devote to the specialised needs of SMEs, particularly first time exporters;
- MEDIA does not have adequate financial and human resources to allocate to the expensive business of overseas promotion of SMEs;
- The risky, costly business of producing for export markets deters individual SMEs from participating.
- SMEs have weak manufacturing capabilities by international standards and are thus forced to produce for the captive home market.

Without further study of this issue, it is extremely difficult to say which of these is the most relevant explanation. However, all of them point to the pressing need to enhance the overseas marketing capabilities of individual and clusters of SMEs, to devote more resources to doing this, and to provide more focussed institutional support. Several policy options seem to present themselves: to create an export development fund for individual and clusters of SMEs, to refocus the role of MEDIA to support them and to encourage the entry of foreign marketing agents around clusters.

The refocusing of MEDIA's role is currently in progress. A consultancy study was recently undertaken on MEDIA's effectiveness by International Development Ireland Ltd.[6] Recently the Government announced its intention to create a specialised Board of Investment to facilitate inward investment. In effect, this means detaching the investment promotion function from MEDIA. Similarly, the industrial estates of MEDIA and DBM could be hived off to the private sector to create an export development fund for SMEs marketing efforts. Large business houses in Mauritius already run industrial estates and the private sector could profitably expand in this direction. Some of the proceeds from future privatisation of public enterprises could be added to increase the size of the export development fund. In contrast with other initiatives, however, little policy attention has been given to date to attracting private sector marketing agents for specific clusters.

[6] Murphy and Suttle (1998).

4.3.3 EXCHANGE RATE MANAGEMENT

Between 1983-1993, Mauritius pursued a managed exchange rate policy under which the Bank of Mauritius intervened on the foreign exchange market to smooth out irregular fluctuations of its currency. An undisclosed basket of currencies of major trading partners is used to determine the value of the Mauritius rupee. The managed float was accompanied by foreign exchange controls. In 1994, foreign exchange controls were fully liberalised. The Exchange Control Act was suspended and free movement of foreign exchange was permitted. Moreover, the Bank of Mauritius stopped setting rates and the rupee was floated with the creation of a new inter-bank foreign exchange market.

In general, private sector analysts have been mixed about the behaviour of the Mauritius currency since the 1994 liberalisation and its influence on exports. One recent report argued that "the rapid depreciation of the rupee over the last year against the major international currencies has certainly lent support to our export industries: but at the same time it has given a blow to our aspirations of becoming a regional and financial business centre" (MCCI, 1998, p. 27). Another recent report argued that "the rupee maintained its downward trend, depreciating sharply vis-à-vis most major currencies ...It is certainly true that Mauritius has a limited capacity to influence international fluctuations. However, it is noteworthy that owing to the inelastic nature of our imports, such a fluctuating rupee is already impacting negatively on our balance of trade" (MEF, 1988, p. 38).

MCCI (1998) and MEF (1998) have focussed on nominal exchange rate changes in their analysis. For our purposes, however, the relevant concept is the real effective exchange rate, which takes into account nominal exchange rates as well as inflation rates between Mauritius and its principal trading partners. Figure 4.2 shows our estimates for the trade weighted real effective exchange rate for Mauritius *vis-à-vis* its three major trading partners – UK, France and USA – for 1994-1998 using IMF data with 1990 as the base year. [7] A fall in the index indicates a real effective exchange rate depreciation and a rise an appreciation. Overall, the rupee depreciated by 6.8% against its major trading partners over 1994-1998. Disaggregation of the data indicates that the rupee appreciated by 4.3% during 1994-1996 and then depreciated sharply by 10.6% during 1996-1998.

In the aftermath of the 1994 liberalisation of the foreign exchange market, the Mauritian real effective exchange rate behaviour was worrying as the country is reliant on labour-cost sensitive export industries like textiles, clothing and footwear. Although a period of sustained real exchange rate appreciation can spur exporters to invest in new equipment and upgrade quality, on balance it seems to have imposed penalties on price sensitive items operating at low margins. In this regard, the real appreciation seems to have negatively affected both established SMEs trying to compete in overseas

---

[7] Figure 4.2 uses the method normally employed by the IMF to determine trading partner weighted real effective exchange rates for Mauritius. The data are from 1994 up to end-June 1998. Yearly average nominal exchange rates are used along with the consumer price index to derive relative prices. Mauritius's three major trading partners are felt to be relevant for the analysis as they accounted for 66% of total exports in 1997. Germany is excluded because it only accounts for a small share of Mauritian exports. Adjusted destination of exports data for 1997 gave the trade weights which were: UK (48.9%), France (29.0%) and USA (22.1%).

Fig 4.2: Trade-Weighted RER, 1994-98

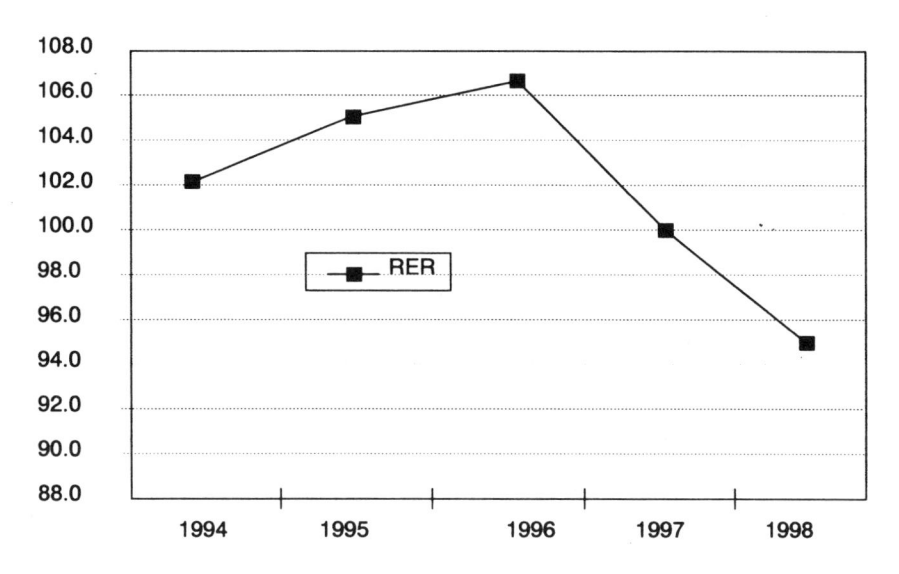

markets and new SME exporters trying to venture out for the first time. Breaking into export markets is a costly and risky undertaking and adverse exchange rate movement adds to uncertainty about future profit streams. In some cases, this may have acted as a net disincentive to exporting and forced a concentration on the home market. This trend was corrected in 1996 and a real depreciation ensured. The significant improvement in incentives to exports is a positive development as far as export-oriented firms in general (and SMEs in particular) are concerned.[8] Experience elsewhere indicates that exports normally respond with a time-lag of one or two years before an improvement occurs in the real exchange rate (as resources take time to shift away from home market based activities into exports). The future challenge for Mauritius is to ensure a period of sustained stability on the foreign exchanges based on a mildly depreciated real exchange rate *vis-à-vis* its main trading partners.

4.3.4. ACCESS TO FINANCE

The Mauritian financial system is reasonbaly well-developed, liberal and market-oriented. Capital market imperfections in the form of financial repression, arbitrary allocation of credit and other interventions in the allocation of resources are minimal by developing country standards. The government seems to adhere to a liberal approach

---
[8] Some analysts in Mauritius argue that a depreciated real exchange rate makes imports more expensive and that this causes adjustment problems to highly import dependent local industries. However, this is typically a short-term issue and a depreciated real exchange rate is a net benefit to the economy. In the medium-term, a competitive real exchange rate provides incentives for import substitution in raw material and component industries and stimulates the formation of industrial clusters and networks in industries like textiles and clothing.

to interest rate determination and rates are responsive to market forces. The financial system is properly regulated by a rejuvenated central bank, the Bank of Mauritius and overly strict rules and procedures do not hamper foreign banks. There are several sources of industrial finance including a network of domestic and offshore financial institutions as well as a fairly active stock market.

The growing offshore financial sector is outward-oriented and typically does not do business with local SMEs. The burden of servicing the credit needs of SMEs falls on the domestic financial sector which consists of about 10 commercial banks (local and foreign-owned), a leasing company and the Development Bank of Mauritius (DBM).[9] The Development Bank of Mauritius – whose operations are examined in more detail in Chapter 5 (Section 5.7) – is the principal public sector provider of concessionary credit to the SME sector. Unfortunately few local SMEs appear to access the stock market or the international capital market which may offer cheaper and more flexible financing than the domestic sector. The country's status as a middle-income country also excludes its firms from accessing the "soft term" small and medium enterprise lending windows of multilateral organisations like the World Bank and the African Development Bank. As in other developing countries, there are many informal sources of finance for small firms in Mauritius such as moneylenders, pawnbrokers, traders, equipment suppliers, friends and relatives.

Despite a liberal financial policy environment and positive institutional developments, there are several problems with industrial finance for SMEs in Mauritius. The Commonwealth mission's interviews with small firms and the Small Scale Entrepreneurs Association of Mauritius (SSEAM) revealed small firms attitudes to (and involvement with) their banks. Some of these issues have been documented in the De Chazal Du Mee (1998) survey of small firms and the SMIDO organised conference on SMEs in 1996 (SMIDO, 1996).

---

[9] Bank of Mauritius (1997) and DBM (1997).

Table 4.2 Commercial Bank Loans and Lending Rates to Small Scale Industries (SSI), 1995-1997 (a)

Year	A Commercial bank Credit to SSI (US$ million)	B Total commercial bank credit to private sector ($ million[10])	C A as a % of B	D Nominal SSI Lending Rate (%)	E Real SSI Lending Rate (%) (b)
1995 June	25.4	1751	1.5	11 to 20	4.9 to 13.9
1996 June	13.9	1605	0.9	11.5 to 20	5.7 to 14.2
1997 June	10.8	1794	0.6	11.5 to 20	3.6 to 12.1
1998 June	10.2	2041.2	0.5	11.5 to 19.5	6.1 to 14.1

Notes: (a) Data refer to SSI engaged in manufacturing, services and trade.
(b) Nominal interest rate adjusted for inflation.
Source: Calculated from Bank of Mauritius (1997 and 1998).

First, on the whole small firms complain about a dearth of commercial bank credit that severely impedes SME start-up, operation, expansion and exporting in Mauritius. This view is borne out by the available data. Table 4.2 provides the latest available information on commercial bank lending to all SMEs (short and long term loans) and the total private sector during mid-1995 to mid-1998. Bank credit to the private sector declined slightly between mid-1995 and mid-1996 but recovered thereafter to exceed $ 2 billion by mid-1998. However, SME credit more than halved from a negligible $25.4 million in mid-1995 to only $10.2 million in mid-1998 (or equivalently from 1.5 % of total bank lending to the private sector to 0.5%). The mid-1998 figure for SME credit translates into an average commercial bank loan size of only $396 to each SME in the country (this is based on the projection in Chapter 2 of an SME and micro-enterprise population of 25,761 establishments). The net result is that SMEs are dependent on non-bank sources for the bulk of their capital requirements.[11]

Second, firms argue that interest rates are very high which, in turn, raises the cost of conducting business and reduces competitiveness. Table 4.2 also shows nominal and real interest rates on commercial bank lending since mid-1995. During the short period, nominal interest rates have been stable, but on the high side (ranging from 11 to 20%). Far more serious is that real interest rates have been high. At the top end of real interest rates, figures have ranged from 12.1% to 14.2%. Our interviews with firms in textiles, printing and IT suggested that the most SMEs were paying at the higher end of real interest rates rather than at the lower end. These are very high by international standards and have constituted a serious drag on SME activity, especially by firms that were

---

[10] Total commercial bank credit to the private sector includes credit to both (formerly) priority and non-priority sectors and credit in the form of investments.
[11] The De Chazal Du Mee (1998) Survey of SMEs found that all firms relied heavily on their own savings, some also obtained loans from friends and relatives and used leasing of equipment and motor vehicles.

unable to tap lower interest sources.[12] The sample SMEs also complained that other non-interest related bank charges were high and few firms saw bank charges as providing good value for money.

Third, firms argue that the other terms of bank loans (repayment periods, guarantees and collateral requirements) were excessive. It indicates that banks are less willing to lend to high-risk/high-return borrowers (reflecting a conservative approach to SME lending by banks). For instance, the De Chazal du Mee (1998) survey reported that 55% of SMEs want few guarantees and 20% want longer repayment periods. Our interviews with SMEs further suggested that there are cases where banks only lent against collateral or that the amount of collateral required to cover a loan is excessive. Moreover, there is a tendency for banks to close down a business "too early" if it gets into difficulties. The nature of banking statistics is such, however, that no hard data is available to back up these claims.

Fourth, firms argue that banks have an "attitude problem" and do not understand small firms. There is little evidence of equity and loan participation by banks, or of systematic provision of business advice by the lender. With notable exceptions, the relationship between banks and SMEs is characterised as an arms-length, detached relationship rather than an intense financial and advisory partnership. The experience of developed economies like the UK suggests that an intense financial and advisory partnership has mutual benefits for borrower and lender alike.[13] For the small business sector many UK banks have appointed specialist advisors in their branches, have implemented extensive programmes of staff training, have sought to improve their communications, and more loan officers have taken to visiting clients in their premises than was the case in the past.

The difficulties faced by SMEs in accessing bank finance and the higher interest rates charged by banks are classic examples of capital market imperfections, which stem from banks and smaller firms having different types of information (the "asymmetric information" problem).[14] Thus, there is a tendency for "large firm bias" in credit allocation by the banking sector. The Government of Mauritius is aware of the problems faced by small firms in accessing bank finance and two proposals were under consideration at the time of the Commonwealth mission:

- Establishment of the Venture Capital Fund to provide long-term risk sharing capital for SMEs and the Mutual Guarantee Fund to act as a guarantor for bank loans to SMEs with insufficient collateral. A detailed plan of action for

---

[12] According to World Bank (1998a), in 1996 Mauritian real interest rates for commercial bank lending were 14% compared with Bangladesh (8%), Sri Lanka (4.8%), India (8.4%), Malaysia (0.8%), Singapore (4.8%), UK (2.8%) and Germany (8.9%). Only African competitors like South Africa (10.3%), Zimbabwe (9.9%) and Madagascar (9.8%) were approaching Mauritian levels. The World Bank defines real interest rates as nominal lending rates adjusted for inflation using the GDP deflator.

[13] See Story (1994) and DTI (1996) for an analysis of the UK experience in this regard.

[14] See Story (1994) for a detailed explanation. In brief – the owner of a small firm has more/better information about the firm than the bank. The existence of asymmetric information, when this favours the SME owner makes the bank more wary of lending to this type of firm. If it does lend, the bank would charge higher interest rates, demand more collateral and have shorter repayment periods than for larger more established firms.

both institutions is contained in a consultancy report prepared by Global Financial Services Ltd (Global Financial Services, undated).

- Creation of a National Entrepreneurs Bank to provide direct financial support to SMEs. This was announced in the 1998 Budget of the Minister of Finance (but no information was available to the Commonwealth mission on its mandate, lending portfolio and operational procedures).

In our view, the Venture Capital/Mutual Guarantee Funds are both valuable institutional additions to SME financial sources and will spur the financial market to deepen and develop in Mauritius. The experience of new financial institutions and services can also be exported as a consultancy service to the African region and other small states. The lack of an intermediary guarantor for SME bank lending is a pressing issue and its creation should receive the highest priority because of its ready impact on the supply of SME finance. Venture capital may take longer to influence the supply of SME finance and may not be available to most SMEs or micro-enterprises. Experience suggests that venture capital is particularly relevant to the high-tech enterprise start-up and growth that is absent in Mauritius. Most of the SME population in Mauritius, however, is confined to the low technology end of manufacturing and services.

Depending on how it is set up, the new National Entrepreneurs Bank is likely to increase the supply of SME finance but, in this market, it will take time for its impact to be felt. Other public action would have a more immediate effect on the supply of SME finance. The state-owned Development Bank of Mauritius (DBM) has long been a concessionary lender to SMEs. It has many strengths including committed staff, a new chief executive, an established brand and a reasonably sized loan portfolio. The DBM's SME lending experience is analysed in Chapter 5 (Section 5.7). Suffice to say, that our enterprise survey and the De Chazal Du Mee (1998) survey suggest that SMEs are dissatisfied with the cumbersome, bureaucratic nature of DBM loan procedures.[15] During our interviews, DBM officials suggested that delays occur because many SMEs do not know how to fill in the loan forms (nor can they provide adequate supporting documents at the onset). The DBM also suggested that as a public sector institution, it has to adopt a cautious lending posture because it is dealing with public money, subject to public sector rules and regulations. The short span of fieldwork in Mauritius meant that the Commonwealth mission was unable to verify either set of claims. However, these claims and counter claims suggest that there may be weaknesses in the public sector provision of concessionary finance to SMEs.

This points to commercialisation of the DBM to improve operational and loan processing efficiency (see Chapter 6 for the details). Our suggestion for the DBM is to remain in the public sector but under different management. A rejuvenated, business-like DBM could play a lead role in promoting exports from individual and clusters of

---

[15] In these surveys a high proportion of enterprises claimed that they have never applied for a DBM loan usually because of lengthy procedures (it can take between 4-6 weeks for processing of loan applications) and a small number said that their applications had been rejected owing to a lack of guarantees.

SMEs. A second option is to stimulate the creation of credit unions in SME associations. This would permit access to small but significant amounts of credit at difficult times.

4.3.5. OTHER POLICIES TO FOSTER LOCAL LINKAGES AND CLUSTERS

Little is known about the nature of intra-firm linkages and clusters in Mauritius. On the issue of supplier linkages, an earlier study undertaken by the Commonwealth Secretariat found that "the local supply base in key industries is weak. As expected, the average local content is high in natural resource based industries like food products (26-50%) but very low in others like textiles and garments (1-25%), electronics (1-10%), and chemicals (1-10%)" (Lall and Wignaraja, 1998, p. 107). The study also found that "there is some sub-contracting activity in the sample. Of the 34 sample firms, about one third seemed to undertake intermittent sub-contracting to SMEs. In textiles and garments, sub-contracting included activities like dying of fabrics, embroidery and sewing. In electronics, it included the manufacture of some parts... in food products, some firms get their labels printed locally" (Lall and Wignaraja, 1998, p. 107). As Chapter 5 shows, the enterprise survey (covering clothing, printing and IT) in the present study confirms the findings of Lall and Wignaraja (1998) that the extent of intra-firm linkages is limited in the Mauritian manufacturing sector.

The few infra-firm linkages between large local firms and SMEs seem to have occurred spontaneously in response to market forces. Until the late 1990s, there were no government policies to encourage sub-contracting, supplier relations or other forms of intra-firm linkages in the Mauritian industrial sector. Import protection based measures like local content rules and public procurement – which were common in East Asia in the 1960s and 1970s to stimulate the local supply industry – are absent in Mauritius. So too are UK or Singapore-style technological upgrading schemes to develop SMEs into efficient industrial suppliers for multinationals/large local conglomerates.

The first time in public policy that some emphasis was given to the issue of intra-firm linkages was in September 1997. A sub-contracting exchange (SUBEX-M) was established with technical assistance from UNIDO along the lines of a model implemented by the UN agency in other developing countries. The Government of Mauritius provided the bulk of the funding for the Mauritian SUBEX but there was also some private sector financing. The main objectives of SUBEX-M are to: (a) create a data bank on potential sub-contractors and customers; (b) provide information on outsourcing possibilities in response to enquires; and (c) provide technical assistance to improve manufacturing capabilities in SMEs on an occasional basis. At the time of the Commonwealth Mission, it had about 80 firms in its data bank and had undertaken a promotional fair in 1997 involving 112 exhibitors as well as 2500 local and international participants. SUBEX had not formally tracked business outcomes from the fair but claims that it resulted in several Mauritian SMEs establishing contracts with Madagascar and the Seychelles.

It is still too early to make a comprehensive evaluation of the success of SUBEX-M.

However, the following preliminary observations can be made about its focus and operations to date:

- ✓ Operations began after a slow start, (there were delays in obtaining funding and hiring qualified engineers) and has yet to make a measurable impact on sub-contracting relations between large firms and SMEs in Mauritius.[16] Also its future was in some doubt at the time of the Commonwealth mission (that in part explains its relatively low take-up rate within the private sector).

- ✓ It has focussed on a group of high skill engineering industries (metal working, plastics, electronics and electrical activities) in which Mauritius has no obvious short or medium-term comparative advantage *vis-à-vis* world markets. Low skill industries, in which the country has an existing and medium-term comparative advantage, as well as some valuable intra-firm linkages are excluded: such as, textiles and clothing, leather products and footwear, and food products. The lack of emphasis given to comparative advantage considerations may in part reflect the agenda of inward-oriented international agencies.

- ✓ It seems to over emphasise *ad hoc* information provision and "match-making" between firms and promotion fairs. The major gap with SUBEX-M is the lack of focussed technical assistance to upgrade existing supplier-relations between large export-oriented enterprises and their suppliers within geographical or sector-specific industrial clusters. In part this may reflect a lack of specialised in-house engineering and technical expertise and inadequate service partnerships with public technology institutions.

The experience gathered from best-practice linkage creation, such as the UK and Singapore, would be valuable for Mauritius. Best practice suggests that focussed assistance, within existing (realistic) marketing chains, is the most efficient means of developing a deep and diverse supplier base in a developing country like Mauritius.[17] By definition such a chain makes products that are in demand in international markets and firms in that chain have reasonable manufacturing capabilities. However, in a world of rapid technological progress and intense competition, survival depends upon technological improvement, quality upgrading and cost-reduction in the SME sector. Best-practice also suggests that success can be achieved when a linkage scheme is private sector driven (supplemented with appropriate inputs from public technology institutions), rather than bureaucrat-led.

In this context, it would be a mistake to shut down SUBEX-M as this would dissipate a valuable learning experience with fostering infra-firm relations. It would also be a mistake to subsidise SUBEX-M to survive independently from the rest of the country's

---

[16] There was a long time lag between the feasibility study that was done in 1994 and implementation of SUBEX-M in Sept. 1997.
[17] Humphrey and Schmitz (1996) and DTI (1996).

technology infrastructure. One option might be to absorb it within SMIDO (this merger would require little restructuring as SUBEX-M is already housed in the SMIDO building in Mauritius). This should be followed by the development of a more focussed linkage programme based on existing marketing chains, a strong private sector orientation and inputs from public technology institutions. SMIDO would need to work with its new partner, MEDIA, to realise success. MEDIA has direct contact with international buyers and knowledge of the price, quality and delivery requirements of international markets while SMIDO knows the characteristics of the SME population.

4.4 Selected Procedural Impediments

4.4.1 THE STATE OF PROCEDURAL OBSTACLES

Previous studies of the Mauritian trade and industrial regime in the 1980s and early 1990s highlighted businesses' transactions costs arising from administrative procedures of the public sector. They documented the reality of a excessive bureaucratic procedures (concerning imports, exports, foreign exchange allocation, foreign investment, taxation and business entry and exit) and its cost to the private sector.[18] Procedures have raised operating costs above optimum levels, wasted valuable management time, employment of additional staff to deal with redundant paperwork, acted as an obstacle to achieving quick response practices, and provided incentives for rent-seeking behaviour by public officials.

To its credit, in the 1990s, the Government of Mauritius began promoting manufacturing efficiency by streamlining and abolishing unnecessary procedures/documents. In 1991 import licensing was abolished. This was soon followed by the elimination of foreign exchange controls in 1994 (foreign exchange transactions no longer needed Bank of Mauritius approval) and a streamlining of foreign investment approvals in 1998 (normal FDI approvals which are eligible for "fast track" processing have a target of 4 weeks while others, a maximum of 12 weeks). There has also been a reduction in processing times for EPZ certificates (from 3-6 months to 1-2 months) and long-term work permits for expatriate technical staff.

Moreover in 1990, in an environment of gradual procedural reform, a One Stop Shop was created within the Ministry of Industry and Commerce to help firms obtain permits/clearances for business start-up and operation. The One Stop Shop operates through a system of liaison officers who are responsible for sorting out enterprises' problems with government departments. Difficult cases are referred to an interministerial committee chaired by the Permanent Secretary or the Minister of Industry and Commerce. In early 1998, SMIDO started a separate One Stop Shop to provide SMEs with information on business start-up and to assist in obtaining permits. SMIDO's

[18] World Bank (1994) and WTO (1995).

One Stop Shop works with the Ministry of Industry and Commerce to provide a follow-up service with specific government departments.

Clearly progress has been achieved in several areas of procedural reform, generally benefiting SMEs. However, the available evidence seems to indicate that procedural reform has not gone far enough even compared to competitors in Africa. A recent survey by the World Economic *Forum's African Competitiveness Report 1998* provides data about the percentage of senior management's time spent negotiating with officials or obtaining licenses, regulations, permits and tax assessments for several African economies including Mauritius. Out of 20 African economies, unexpectedly Mauritius is ranked 14th by this measure of procedural inefficiency. Mauritian enterprise senior management spends up to 13% of their time dealing with permits/other regulatory issues compared with only 3% in Namibia, 4% Botswana, 7% South Africa, 10% Tunisia, 11% Uganda and 12% Cote d'Ivoire. Although cross-country comparisons of procedural inefficiency are often subjective and difficult to make, they can provide a useful perspective.

4.4.2 SMALL BUSINESS START-UP PROBLEMS

One important area, which seems to have escaped serious procedural reform in Mauritius, is regulations on business start-up. [19] Regulatory costs are much more damaging to small businesses than to large firms. Focused on an owner/manager, small firms lack specialist staff to obtain multiple permits/clearances. They have less political influence than large firms to by-pass bureaucratic obstacles. Compared to large firms, they can ill afford the foregone output associated with delays to project execution or to pay rents connected with multiple clearances.

Our survey of SMEs suggests it takes an average of 7 months to overcome the bureaucratic hurdles to start a small business in Mauritius. [20] The removal of a few outliners (with processing times in excess of 24 months) reduces the average to 4.2 months. These averages mask a wide variation in bureaucratic processing times for small firm start-up in the sample. The detailed results show that at best, it takes between 0-3 months while at worst it can be more than 10 months (see Figure 4.3). The 0-3 month processing times is probably an acceptable delay to small firm start-up. However, the worst case results are very high processing times by international standards and can retard the rate of SME start-up in the country. These results are a central concern for policy action.

The cost of procedures associated with new firm start-up is difficult to estimate in monetary terms but the opportunity costs are clear: *the owner/senior manager of a typical*

---

[19] For instance, data provided by SMIDO shows that its One Stop Shop dealt with about 200 enquiries from small firms during February-July 1998. Many of these requested information on establishing businesses (e.g. where to get loans, what to produce or where equipment to buy) but a significant share (9%) concerned problems with getting start-up permits from national/local government organs.

[20] Results from the first set of 17 responses received suggested a 7.8 months figure but adding the results from an additional 8 responses recently received, the figure fell to about 7 months.

small firm spends about 8.5% of his/her time each month dealing with taxes and other government regulations/officials.[21]

Fig 4.3: Time to Obtain All Permits to Start-up

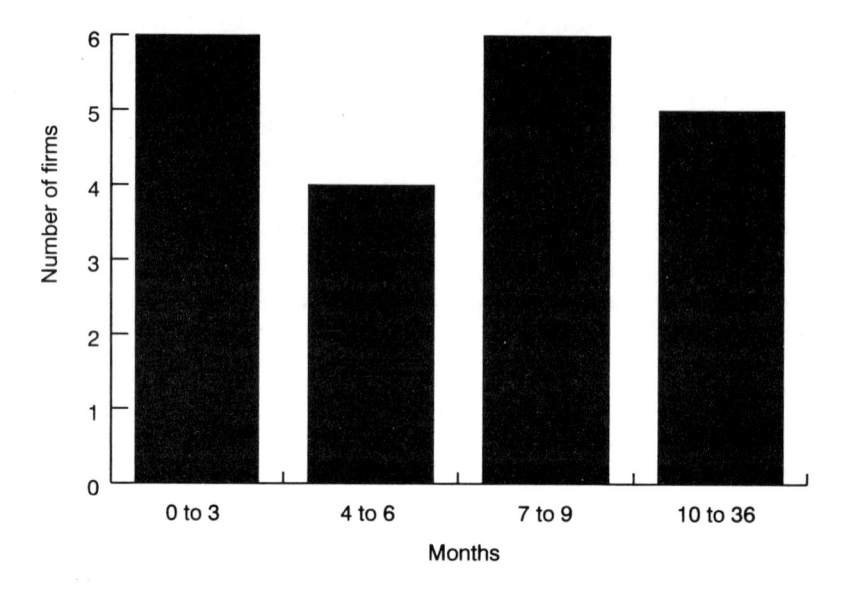

[Bar chart showing Number of firms vs Months:
- 0 to 3: 6
- 4 to 6: 4
- 7 to 9: 6
- 10 to 36: 5]

The list of permits/clearances required for setting up an enterprise in Mauritius including an SME is contained in Appendix 2. A plethora of permits/clearances are required for start-up including: development/buildings permits, local authority permits, electric motor permits, applications for foreign investment, work permits, residence permits, water supply applications, electricity supply applications, telephone/fax applications and national pension fund registration.[22] It is worth remembering that once a firm is established there are many regulations governing business operation (these range from labour laws and environmental standards to accessing duty-free raw materials and payment of taxes).

Figure 4.4 provides enterprise impressions of relative difficulties faced in obtaining 11 different start-up permits for small firms from the Commonwealth SME survey. A score of 5 indicates the most difficult permits to obtain and 1 indicates the least difficult. The following picture emerges from the survey data and detailed interviews with the two One Stop Shops and small firms:

---

[21] Estimate from the Commonwealth SME survey for this study. It is the Mission's judgement that this may be closer to the real situation than the figure for Mauritius in the African Competitiveness Report 1998. However, our figure remains higher than the most efficient African economies.
[22] Ministry of Industry and Commerce (1998).

- The most difficult permits are those affecting residence and work. This is paradoxical because Mauritius has an open door policy towards foreign investment but has traditionally discouraged the import of foreign workers (or engineering technical staff) in favour of local employment. There is an assumption that the requisite (right quality) skills are available locally which may not be so for high-level engineering and technical skills. For a small island, these approvals are gained within a cumbersome structure. Residence permits, for expatriate staff and foreign investors, are granted by the Passport and Immigration Office and work permits by the Ministry of Education & Human Resource Development. An inter-ministerial committee is usually involved and approval is required from the Prime Minister's Office. The process can take from 1-3 months. Approval times are faster for EPZ firms than for non-EPZ firms. Expatriates are normally granted a two-year permit and the firm has to pay a financial bond of Rs. 50,000 and produce a return ticket. Extensions are difficult and workers are sometimes sent home, only to be brought back later. All of this adds to the transactions costs of firms, particularly SMEs.[23]

- A close second is foreign investment applications. This finding is supported by a previous Commonwealth Secretariat study which found that it can take between 9-32 weeks to obtain foreign investment approval in Mauritius because of a multi-stage approval process with excessive documentation requirements.[24] Falling inward investment in the mid-1990s resulted in an overhaul of these procedures. A powerful Board of Investment was announced in 1998 along with targets for processing times for FDI approvals. However, at the time of the Commonwealth mission, the Board of Investment had not yet been established and it was unclear whether the targets for processing times had come into effect. This may continue to be a problem for small firms seeking joint ventures with foreign investors.

- Obtaining local government permits (e.g. development/building, local authority and fire services) is also very time consuming and bureaucratic. Three separate permits are required for construction, building and business operation from the same local authority. Before the issue of the operating permit, the local authority requires further clearance from five different government departments (Ministry of Health, Ministry of the Environment, Ministry of Labour and Industrial Relations, Fire Services and Police Department). All these steps are compulsory and the documentation requirements are excessive. Co-ordination between the different departments

---

[23] Our interviews with the One Stop Shop suggest that work permits for foreign production managers had become easier than in the past. Today One Stop Shop can assist a firm to get a temporary entry visa, which is granted in 3 days. After processing by an inter-departmental committee, the work permit is issued within 2-3 months.

[24] Lall and Wignaraja (1998).

is weak and the process, from start to finish, can take from 2-12 months. Particular problems seem to arise when a firm is located in a residential zone but somewhat less difficult for firms which are in designated industrial zones. The application of health, environmental and fire safety standards seem to be particularly slow and restrictive.

Fig 4.4: Start-up Permit Problems

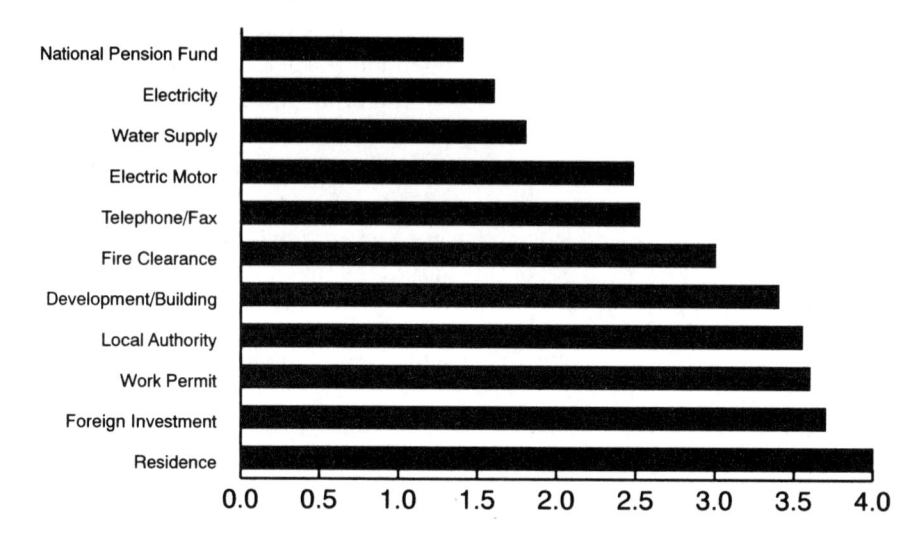

Category	Value
National Pension Fund	1.5
Electricity	1.6
Water Supply	1.8
Electric Motor	2.5
Telephone/Fax	2.5
Fire Clearance	3.0
Development/Building	3.4
Local Authority	3.5
Work Permit	3.6
Foreign Investment	3.7
Residence	4.0

- Compared with many other developing countries, utility applications (telephones, water supply and electricity) are relatively easy to process in Mauritius. A major improvement has occurred in telephone application processing times, which range from only 1-4 weeks. In any case, easy access to mobile telephones has diffused this problem. Water and electricity applications are usually processed in three weeks but small firms in geographically remote areas can face delays of 3-4 months. This is more of a problem of infrastructure gaps rather than cumbersome bureaucratic procedures *per se*.

- National Pension Fund registration with the Ministry of Social Security poses the least problems to small firms.

Quite apart from the transactions costs involved in business start-up due to excessive administrative procedures, an important problem concerning administrative obstacles in Mauritius is the uncertainty of the outcome. Small firms begin processes without knowing how and when they will end. The time and cost vary from firm to firm depending on contacts, familiarity with bureaucratic processes, financial resources available for payments to bureaucrats and linkages with political groups. Experience from developed and developing countries suggests that entry procedures are an important influence on the rate of small business start-up. Where bureaucratic barriers to start-up are significant, they can act as a disincentive to new small firm creation and growth.

4.5 Infrastructure Impediments

The influence of infrastructure impediments on private sector activity has been considered by several recent studies and the Government of Mauritius is well aware of the nature of the problem.[25] Few further insights can be added to existing knowledge by this study. Figure 4.5 shows small firm perspectives on the degree of difficulty caused by different aspects of infrastructure in Mauritius from the Commonwealth enterprise survey. A score of 5 indicates the most difficult permits to obtain and 1 indicates the most straightforward.

The data reinforce previous findings that the cost and availability of air freight is a major barrier to small firm exporting in Mauritius. This is closely followed by firms having difficulties in acquiring land or industrial space and weaknesses in electricity supply, in the form of both voltage fluctuations and breakdowns. Customs clearance is also regarded as a problem by some small firms, but in contrast with concerns about air freight, sea freight cost and availability this does not pose a serious problem. Other aspects of Mauritian infrastructure are considered quite efficient by small firms (e.g. water supply and sewage, airport facilities and telecommunications reliability).

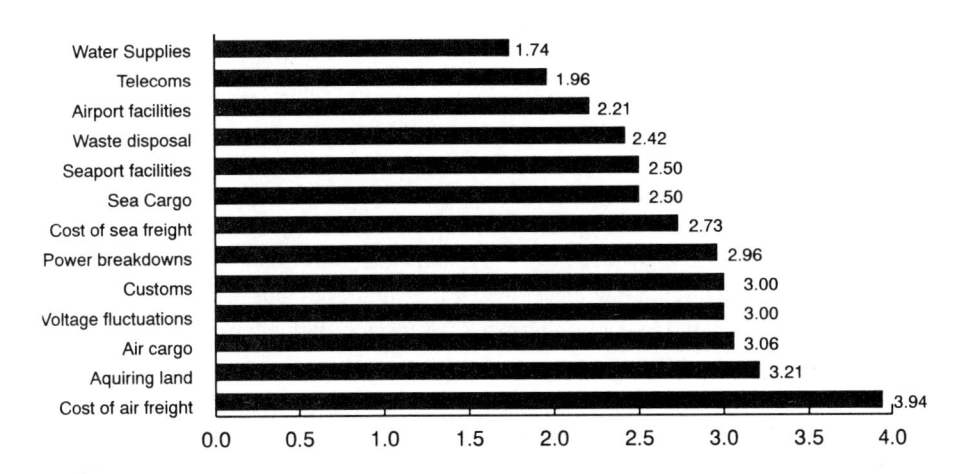

Fig 4.5: Infrastructure Problems

Category	Score
Water Supplies	1.74
Telecoms	1.96
Airport facilities	2.21
Waste disposal	2.42
Seaport facilities	2.50
Sea Cargo	2.50
Cost of sea freight	2.73
Power breakdowns	2.96
Customs	3.00
Voltage fluctuations	3.00
Air cargo	3.06
Aquiring land	3.21
Cost of air freight	3.94

[25] World Bank (1994), MEDRC (1997); Lall and Wignaraja (1998); De Chazal du Mee (1998).

4.6. Conclusions

This chapter examined the influence of the Mauritian macroeconomic, trade and industrial policy environment on small firm operation and the attainment of international competitiveness. Following a ranking by small firms of the degree of obstacle presented by individual policies and procedures, the analysis examined selected policy, procedural and infrastructural impediments to competitiveness in more detail.

The overall conclusion is that the present policy environment is now more favourable to small firms than it was previously due to two decades of gradual liberalisation and deregulation of government controls. The country was fortunate to have escaped a strong or prolonged inward-orientation, which hampered many developing countries since the 1960s and 1970s. The Mauritian policy environment is more open and small business-friendly than those of many competitors in Africa and the Indian Sub-Continent. Economic policy is generally well managed and more predictable than most. The private sector is consulted before major policy initiatives are implemented and their views often shape policy. Major areas of policy success include switching from quantitative restrictions to tariffs (and cuts in tariffs), the lack of public procurement and local content rules, maintaining a depreciated real exchange rate, removal of exchange controls, maintaining a liberal and market-oriented banking system, the introduction of VAT, and streamlining some administrative procedures. This is an impressive record and makes Mauritian enterprises more poised than others to reap future gains from globalisation of trade and investment.

However despite past successes in policy reform, there is still room for improvement, which in turn will benefit small firms as well as the rest of the Mauritian private sector. Tariff reform is far from complete and the existing protective structure discriminates against small firms, particularly those in the non-EPZ sector. The future agenda on tariff reform is unclear. Small firms lack ready access to duty-free imported inputs to offset an anti-export bias in the trade regime. Until relatively recently, there was little effective overseas marketing support for small firms. MEDIA has improved service delivery in this regard but the take-up rate among small firms has been quite low. This raises questions about the quantity and quality of the services provided. Small firms face higher real interest rates, more restrictive terms and less access to commercial bank finance than large firms (which indicates a "large firm bias" in the allocation of finance). There is an absence of effective policies to develop linkages and industrial clusters among small firms. SUBEX-M – the only scheme which provides information about potential intra-firm production linkages – started very recently but has run into difficulties with the phasing out of technical assistance from an international donor. There are serious administrative barriers to small firm start-up which raise SMEs' transaction costs above those of competitor economies. Start-up procedures have raised operating costs above optimum levels, wasted scarce management time, employment of additional staff to deal with redundant paperwork, acted as an obstacle to efforts to adopt quick response practices, and provided incentives for rent-seeking behaviour by public officials. Long processing delays arise from a multi-stage approval process involving contact with numerous public agencies.

5 The Institutional Support System for SMEs

5.1 Introduction

This chapter aims to outline briefly the public sector institutional support system for SMEs. It covers the major providers of marketing, design, technology, finance and training services for SMEs. It focuses on SMIDO, EPZDA, MEDIA and IVTB, and, to a lesser extent, DBM.[1] The review of public SME institutions does not offer a comprehensive picture of individual agencies. This is a separate exercise which requires considerable funding, lengthy fieldwork and specialised technical manpower.[2] Instead, the chapter aims to synthesise and analyse small enterprise perceptions in four areas: (a) the level and awareness of SME services; (b) the degree of take-up; (c) the quality of service delivery; and (d) future service needs. Based on these findings, consultancy studies of SME institutions, annual reports of SME institutions and our interviews with individual institutions, the chapter assesses the effectiveness of the public SME system as a whole.

5.2. Background on the SME Support System

Table 5.1 provides the available background data on the five public sector institutions, which provide services to SMEs (including their objective, major services, number of staff and budget). The five institutions vary considerably in purpose, size (measured by the number of staff and financial resource base), and age:

- SMIDO deals exclusively with SMEs and offers information, training and other services. The other four assist both small and large enterprises yet each has a different entry point to service delivery. EPZDA provides consultancy and information services. MEDIA acts as a trade promotion agency and runs industrial estates. IVTB focuses on training and related services while DBM is a traditional development bank with soft loans and some business advice.

- Of the five institutions, DBM and IVTB are the largest in terms of their financial resource base and employment. SMIDO and EPZDA (similar in terms of employment and financial resources) are the smallest. MEDIA falls in between these extremes.

---

[1] During our fieldwork in Mauritius, time constraints prevented our examining the contribution made to SME service provision by other public agencies such as the Mauritius Bureau of Standards and the University of Mauritius. However, the agencies we selected provide the bulk of services to SMEs in the country. A handful of private sector SME providers exist (e.g the Mauritius Employers Federation and consultancy firms) but these are beyond the scope of the study.
[2] Murphy and Suttle (1998) made this kind of detailed assessment on MEDIA.

Table 5.1: Overview of Institutions Supporting SMEs (most recent estimates)

Institutions	Core purpose	Major services
SMIDO	To provide support to small and medium-sized manufacturing enterprises in order to enhance their competitiveness	Entrepreneurship Development Programme One-Stop Shop Consultancy Awards Documentation Centre Common Facilities Centre Training
EPZDA	To provide support to all enterprises operating within the Export Processing Zone	Consultancy Training Trend Forum Publications Information services lothing Technology Centre User Group
MEDIA	To promote exports To promote foreign direct investment To develop and operate industrial sites and estates	Trade Information Centre Buyer/seller meets Trade fairs MITEX Market surveys Industrial estates
IVTB	The promotion, development and delivery of training	Training courses Administration of training levy refund Technical advice Library and information services
DBM	To provide finance to small and medium enterprises	Loans Business advice Industrial estates

Sources: SMIDO Annual Report, 1995/96; EPZDA Annual Report, 1996/97; MEDIA Export Directory, 1998/99; MEDIA Action Plan, 1996; Study on Activities of MEDIA, Murphy and Suttle (1998); IVTB Directory,1998; Interviews with the Government of Mauritius in mid-1998.

- In existence since the 1970s, DBM is probably the oldest of the five institutions. MEDIA, founded next, is nearly fifteen years old. SMIDO, EPZDA and IVTB are all less than eight years old.
- With the exception of the DBM, the other agencies come under the preview

5 The Institutional Support System for SMEs

5.1 Introduction

This chapter aims to outline briefly the public sector institutional support system for SMEs. It covers the major providers of marketing, design, technology, finance and training services for SMEs. It focuses on SMIDO, EPZDA, MEDIA and IVTB, and, to a lesser extent, DBM.[1] The review of public SME institutions does not offer a comprehensive picture of individual agencies. This is a separate exercise which requires considerable funding, lengthy fieldwork and specialised technical manpower.[2] Instead, the chapter aims to synthesise and analyse small enterprise perceptions in four areas: (a) the level and awareness of SME services; (b) the degree of take-up; (c) the quality of service delivery; and (d) future service needs. Based on these findings, consultancy studies of SME institutions, annual reports of SME institutions and our interviews with individual institutions, the chapter assesses the effectiveness of the public SME system as a whole.

5.2. Background on the SME Support System

Table 5.1 provides the available background data on the five public sector institutions, which provide services to SMEs (including their objective, major services, number of staff and budget). The five institutions vary considerably in purpose, size (measured by the number of staff and financial resource base), and age:

- SMIDO deals exclusively with SMEs and offers information, training and other services. The other four assist both small and large enterprises yet each has a different entry point to service delivery. EPZDA provides consultancy and information services. MEDIA acts as a trade promotion agency and runs industrial estates. IVTB focuses on training and related services while DBM is a traditional development bank with soft loans and some business advice.

- Of the five institutions, DBM and IVTB are the largest in terms of their financial resource base and employment. SMIDO and EPZDA (similar in terms of employment and financial resources) are the smallest. MEDIA falls in between these extremes.

---

[1] During our fieldwork in Mauritius, time constraints prevented our examining the contribution made to SME service provision by other public agencies such as the Mauritius Bureau of Standards and the University of Mauritius. However, the agencies we selected provide the bulk of services to SMEs in the country. A handful of private sector SME providers exist (e.g the Mauritius Employers Federation and consultancy firms) but these are beyond the scope of the study.
[2] Murphy and Suttle (1998) made this kind of detailed assessment on MEDIA.

Table 5.1: Overview of Institutions Supporting SMEs (most recent estimates)

Institutions	Core purpose	Major services
SMIDO	To provide support to small and medium-sized manufacturing enterprises in order to enhance their competitiveness	Entrepreneurship Development Programme
		One-Stop Shop
		Consultancy
		Awards
		Documentation Centre
		Common Facilities Centre
		Training
EPZDA	To provide support to all enterprises operating within the Export Processing Zone	Consultancy
		Training
		Trend Forum
		Publications
		Information services
		lothing Technology Centre
		User Group
MEDIA	To promote exports	Trade Information Centre
	To promote foreign direct investment	Buyer/seller meets
	To develop and operate industrial sites and estates	Trade fairs
		MITEX
		Market surveys
		Industrial estates
IVTB	The promotion, development and delivery of training	Training courses
		Administration of training levy refund
		Technical advice
		Library and information services
DBM	To provide finance to small and medium enterprises	Loans
		Business advice
		Industrial estates

Sources: SMIDO Annual Report, 1995/96; EPZDA Annual Report, 1996/97; MEDIA Export Directory, 1998/99; MEDIA Action Plan, 1996; Study on Activities of MEDIA, Murphy and Suttle (1998); IVTB Directory,1998; Interviews with the Government of Mauritius in mid-1998.

- In existence since the 1970s, DBM is probably the oldest of the five institutions. MEDIA, founded next, is nearly fifteen years old. SMIDO, EPZDA and IVTB are all less than eight years old.

- With the exception of the DBM, the other agencies come under the preview

Number of staff	Financial Resource Base	Date of establishment
43	Rs14.2m Government grant for 1998/99	1993
31	Rs20m Government grant for 1996/97 Revenue generated:Rs6.5m	1992
58	Rs55m Government grant or 1998/99	1985
500+	Rs100m Government grant for 1998/99	1992
250	Investment portfolio Rs2.4 billion– no grant	1970s

of the Ministry of Industry and Commerce (MOIC). These agencies have some autonomy in day-to-day matters but function under the strategic guidance of the MOIC.

5.3 Enterprise Perceptions of SME Institutions

5.3.1 SMIDO

Purpose and Target Market

The Small and Medium Industry Development Organisation (SMIDO), in its current form, was given its mandate by The Industrial Expansion Act of 1993. SMIDO is charged with providing support to indigenous enterprises that:

- are engaged in manufacturing
- use production equipment which does not exceed 10 million Mauritian Rupees (in 1993).

These enterprises may, or may not, be actively engaged in exporting. It does not support foreign-owned small firms. The broad mission of SMIDO is to enhance the competitiveness of SMEs "...with a view to creating a modern, strong, efficient and export-oriented SME sector in the country."

The principal reason for an SME to register with SMIDO is to achieve exemption from the payment of duties or levies on the importation of production equipment. Registration with SMIDO also gives SMEs preferential access to a range of services (including training, information, marketing assistance and export support).

The current definition of SMEs excludes companies operating within the service sector and, as such, prevents them from benefiting from the services offered by SMIDO. Given that the service sector is increasingly acknowledged as an engine of both domestic and export growth, and that substantial opportunities exist for indirect exporting through inter-company linkages and the provision of services to exporters, we recommend a more inclusive definition of SMEs.

Services

SMIDO offers a range of services, the major ones being:

The Entrepreneurship Development Programme – for potential entrepreneurs, this programme consists primarily of workshops on skills required to launch and manage a small firm.

The One-Stop Shop – A service facility with the purpose of helping entrepreneurs expedite the start-up of small enterprises. It provides assistance in negotiating the formalities of registration and making applications for relevant licences.

Consultancy services – Although SMIDO provides virtually no consultancy services itself, it endeavours to source and match external consultants with SMEs.

Awards – SMIDO runs three award schemes: the Small Enterprise Project Award given to young people for a viable project proposal; the Technology Award for the use of innovation in product or process; and the Export Award given for achievements in exports.

The Documentation Centre – This is an information resource centre for business and market knowledge. Information is mainly in the form of journals, magazines, books, and access to the Internet.

The Common Facilities Centre – This is a technical workshop with trained staff. Members of SMIDO can use this facility on an ad hoc basis or participate in a range of technical courses run in the workshop.

Training courses – Training courses on a wide range of management and technical topics are run on a regular basis.

User Perceptions of Services

Table 5.2: User Perceptions of SMIDO Services

(23 responses)	% Heard of	% Used	Useful
Entrepreneurship Development Programme	74	17	4
One Stop Shop	74	22	3.4
Consultancy services	57	9	4.5
Awards	48	0	–
Documentation Centre	61	9	3
Common Facilities Centre	61	4	5
Training courses	91	43	3.4
Overall average	**67**	**15**	**3.9**

In our survey, we asked respondents about whether they had "heard of" and "used" a number of SMIDO services. If the service had been used, we also asked how useful they found it. Twenty-three enterprises responded to these questions and the aggregate results are shown below. Note that the grading of "usefulness" is the arithmetic mean of responses given on a scale of 1 to 5, where 1 = not useful and 5 = very useful.

The aggregate results give a clear picture of levels of awareness and take-up, and perceptions of usefulness (see Table 5.2). Within the sample, it is textile companies that are making most use of SMIDO services, although high levels of awareness exist in both of the other sectors. 91% of respondents had heard of the training courses that SMIDO offers, and 74% of respondents were aware of both the One Stop Shop and the Entrepreneurship Development Programme. Lower levels of awareness exist of the other services, particularly the consultancy services and the Awards. However, in our sample the use of all of these services (apart from training) is especially low. None of the sample used the Awards, only 4% had used the Common Facilities Centre and 9% had taken advantage of the consultancy services and the Documentation Centre.

Perceptions of usefulness are favourable (although these may reflect perceptions rather than actual usage). There appear to be no studies assessing the impact of the SMIDO interventions in terms of the overall objectives for the provision of these services.

When our sample was asked what other services they would like to see SMIDO offer, the responses included:

- **help in finding markets and buyers** – this was mentioned by three respondents, who suggested that SMIDO might set up buyer/seller meets or organise trade fairs and exhibitions.

- **sector- or function-specific courses** – suggestions were made for courses designed for the printing industry and courses on import and export documentation.

- **assistance in obtaining duty-free access to raw materials** – this was cited by four companies and is obviously a concern of non-EPZ companies.

- **availability of technicians to repair machines on a 24-hour basis** – one respondent suggested that SMIDO might provide such a service.

It is interesting to note that, in the main, these services are outside the mandate of SMIDO and some are provided by other organisations (e.g. MEDIA for buyer/seller meets). In our view, this indicates that the SME population might be confused about which types of services are (or should be offered) by the various SME support institutions. In our view, these suggestions indicate a desire for assistance to be as specific and practical as possible. Both of these issues are addressed in our proposals contained in Chapter 6.

5.3.2 EPZDA

Purpose and Target Market

The Export Processing Zone Development Authority (EPZDA) was established in 1992 to provide a range of services to EPZ firms in order to improve their competitiveness. With its principal focus on the smaller exporter, to some extent it overlaps with the target population of SMIDO.

Because of the nature of export development in Mauritius, most of the companies registered with EPZDA are in the textile industry and, in response to their needs, EPZDA has developed a comprehensive range of support services for this industry. As a result, EPZDA is now clearly perceived in the SME marketplace as servicing the textile industry and having little relevance to other sectors.

EPZDA is currently trying to extend its reach to other sectors, in particular the IT industry, but may be hampered by a lack of credibility due to its established positioning in textiles. Additionally, limited access to resources may inhibit its development of expertise in other sectors.

Services

The key services offered by EPZDA are:

Consultancy services – EPZDA facilitates customised consultancy on an individual firm basis, with the focus predominantly on technical or production issues, for example, pattern making, handling systems, quality control and procedures.

Trend Forum – This is an occasional event comprising seminars and workshops, exhibitions and buyer/seller meets, all revolving around the textile industry. Major inputs are provided by well-established local companies and experts from abroad.

Publications – The principal publication is "Industry Focus", a bi-monthly magazine. This is a joint publication of the Ministry of Industry and Commerce, EPZDA, MEDIA, SMIDO and the Mauritius Standards Bureau. It covers general business topics, news and provides technical support, primarily for the textile industry.

Training courses – Most of the training courses operate as technical workshops, covering a wide range of practical issues of the textile industry.

Research and development projects – Working with foreign consultants, EPZDA runs projects tackling current issues mainly in the textile industry

Information services – These are focused on the Information and Resource Centre, which aims to provide a paper-based information centre, and the Web service, an internet-based information exchange that can be accessed by both members and non-members.

Clothing Technology Centre – A dedicated building providing a resource centre for product development and R&D in the textile industry. Members are able to rent time in order to become better acquainted with new technologies such as CAD/CAM.

The User Scheme – This is a structured framework for supporting EPZDA members, especially SMEs. Members are provided regularly with a range of meetings, seminars and open sessions.

User Perceptions of Services

As with SMIDO, we tried to evaluate the take-up and effectiveness of the services offered by EPZDA. Twenty-one enterprises responded to these questions and the aggregate results are shown in Table 5.3.

Table 5.3: User Perceptions of EPZDA Services

(21 responses)	% Heard of	% Used	Useful
Consultancy services	62	24	4.2
Trend Forum	86	19	4
Publications	76	33	3.9
Training courses	81	24	4.6
Information services	71	14	4
Clothing Technology Centre	62	24	4.8
The User Group	43	24	4.8
Overall average	**69**	**23**	**4.3**

The majority of SMEs using EPZDA are in the textile industry. Overall, there appears to be a slightly higher levels of awareness and usage of EPZDA's activities than those of some other organisations. Perceptions of usefulness are favourable, especially the Clothing Technology Centre and the User Group. Respondents also perceived the training courses and the consultancy services to be particularly useful.

Other services that were of interest to SMEs included:[3]

- *servicing the printing and publishing industry* – one respondent considered that EPZDA was doing a good job for the textile industry and that this should be extended to his own industry.

- *strategic business planning* – this was cited by one respondent.

- *assistance with international trade shows, especially the airfreighting of exhibition equipment* – this constituted a request for financial help for SMEs.

5.3.3 MEDIA

Purpose and Target Market

MEDIA is essentially an agency with the two objectives of encouraging inward investment and promoting Mauritian exports. Its third area of activity is the establishment of industrial sites primarily to facilitate inward investment, but also to supplement gaps in the activities of the commercial property development industry.

MEDIA has attained a high profile from its past successes in attracting foreign investment and in promoting the exports of a few large Mauritian companies. Although it declares that its services are appropriate to the SME sector, it generally engages in activities, such as international trade fairs, that are outside the scope of the average small business. It is biased towards the textile industry, where it overlaps with EPZDA.

---

[3] One SME suggested that no services were of interest because "EPZDA is only available to big firms". This may be indicative of the overall perception of EPZDA amongst SMEs that it is a successful organisation but mainly helps large textile firms.

It is doubtful that MEDIA can, with its current portfolio of support services, maximise its effectiveness for both the large-scale and the small-scale business in Mauritius. This point was also made in a comprehensive assessment of MEIDA by International Development Ireland Ltd (Murphy and Suttle, 1998).

Services

The principal services offered by MEDIA are:

Trade Information Centre – a paper-based resource centre for business information, covering a wide number of industries and markets.

Buyer/seller meets and contact promotion programmes – events and activities held in Mauritius or in overseas markets, designed to bring together buyers and sellers in specific industries and to promote specific products.

Trade fairs – participation in international trade fairs organised on a group basis.

MITEX/MIATEX – The Mauritius International Textile Exhibition is held annually in Mauritius. The Mauritius International Apparel and Textile Exhibition held in Paris and London.

Market surveys – MEDIA commissions surveys on export opportunities in specific overseas markets.

Industrial estates – MEDIA builds, owns and manages 100,000 sq. metres of industrial space in Mauritius, including a special 'intelligent' building for the IT sector.

In addition, MEDIA has promotion offices in France, UK, India and Kenya, with more limited representation in the US, and a number of COMESA countries.

User Perceptions of Services

The aggregate results of our survey of SMEs on their perceptions of the services offered by MEDIA are shown in Table 5.4. Twenty-two enterprises responded to these questions.

Table 5.4: User Perceptions of MEDIA Services

(22 responses)	% Heard of	% Used	Useful
Trade Information Centre	68	9	4
Buyer/seller meets	73	36	3.9
Trade fairs	91	14	3.7
MITEX	73	0	–
Market surveys	64	14	2.5
Industrial estates	68	9	5
Overall average	**73**	**14**	**3.8**

Awareness of MEDIA's activities is generally high, particularly of the trade fairs, which registered a 91% awareness rate. However, apart from the buyer/seller meets, take-up is low amongst the SME sector, even though those companies that do use MEDIA's services are spread more evenly across the industry sectors than for SMIDO and EPZDA. Our discussions with companies revealed that, for many, the cost of participating in overseas trade fairs and exhibitions is prohibitively high. The buyer/seller meets are much more affordable, but the perception of their usefulness is highly dependent on the outcome. If a transaction results, then the participating firm would consider the activity to be useful. If no business was gained or if contacts were made but no sales resulted directly, then the meet might be perceived as not useful or only marginally useful.

The value of the market surveys was perceived as relatively low, but we would suggest that perception is largely a function of how well the information was used or incorporated into the SME firm. It requires experience and skill to maximise the use of market information, and these capabilities are often lacking in SMEs.

Although only 9% of the sample made use of the industrial estates facility these companies recorded 100% satisfaction.

Additional comments from the survey respondents included:

- *industrial estates appropriate to SME resources* – this was cited by two companies who considered the existing provision to be beyond the resources of most SMEs.

- *financial assistance for SMEs to participate in international exhibitions or trade fairs* – was requested by one company.

Overall SMEs perceive MEDIA as an organisation which is geared to meeting the needs of larger companies. The small business entrepreneur cannot usually afford the time or money to participate in international exhibitions or fairs. Here, undoubtedly, is a role either for an industry association or a commercial export house to participate in a trade fair on behalf of a consortium of SME exporters. Although we understand that MEDIA itself has attempted to do this, we would suggest that an organisation with more of a vested interest would have the motivation to achieve better results.

5.3.4 IVTB

Purpose and Target Market

Whilst not directly mandated to provide support to the SME sector, the Industrial and Vocational Training Board (IVTB) provides a range of educational courses that complement the activities of both EPZDA and SMIDO. The training levy imposed on all companies links IVTB to the SME support infrastructure. Within this scheme, companies are required to contribute a percentage of their wage costs to a centralised fund. When a company sends an employee on an approved training course, it can claim a part refund of the course fee. This is funded by the training levy. Both IVTB and commercial training organisations run approved courses. However, the take-up of the training levy refund is disappointingly low.

Services

IVTB is mandated with the following tasks:

- Planning, monitoring and evaluation of training programmes
- Design and development of training curricula
- Implementation of training schemes and programmes
- Financing of training of school leavers and employees through a levy/grant system.

As of 1998, 90 private training institutions were registered with the IVTB, including 10 in-house training centres. In addition, IVTB operates 18 of its own Training Centres. To help the development of appropriate training courses, Training Advisory Committees exist to service 21 industry sectors. IVTB also provides library and information services and technical advice.

User Perceptions of Services

22 SMEs responded to questions about their use of IVTB services' training courses, their use of the training levy refund, technical advice and library and information services. See Table 5.5.

Table 5.5: User Perceptions of IVTB Services

(22 responses)	% Heard of	% Used	Useful
Training courses	95	36	3.8
Training levy refund	86	32	4.1
Technical advice	50	0	–
Library and information services	27	0	–
Overall average	65	17	4.0

Once again, it is mainly the textile sector that makes use of IVTB's services. There is an exceptionally high level of awareness of IVTB as a training provider and administrator of the training levy refund, but relatively low awareness of its other activities. The use of the training courses and the training levy refund is consistent with IVTB's own research. Where companies have used IVTB's training, the overall perception of usefulness is relatively high. Though none of our sample had used IVTB's technical advice or information service.

Some respondents would like IVTB to offer more industry-specific skill-based workshops and courses that could be scheduled outside working hours. Discussions with interviewees, especially in the printing and pre-press industry, indicated that some teaching was very out-of-date and that courses failed to produce graduates with the required skills.

5.3.5 DBM

Purpose and Target Market

The Development Bank of Mauritius was established expressly to provide the small business with finance at an affordable rate of interest. Typically the interest rate set by DBM is around 10%, compared with the usual rate of 16% charged by the commercial banks.[4]

User Perceptions of Services

Two activities of the DBM – loans and business advice – are assessed in the survey, selected as being the most relevant to SMEs. The responses of 23 companies are aggregated and are shown in Table 5.6.

Table 5.6: User Perceptions of DBM Services

(23 responses)	% Heard of	% Used	Useful
Loans	100	30	4.7
Business advice	35	0	–
Overall average	**68**	**15**	**4.7 (a)**

Note: (a) this scoring is based on the evaluation of one service only

Whilst all of our sample are aware of DBM's role, the uptake of its finance facilities is surprisingly low. Several of our respondents declared loans taken out from commercial banks at a much higher rate of interest. The reasons for this are not clear and should be investigated more thoroughly, but some of the comments reveal a significant level of dissatisfaction with the service provided by DBM.

Criticisms mainly revolve around the lending criteria, fairness in granting funds, the slow processing of applications and the refusal to lend against second-hand machinery. The principal criterion for lending is to secure a high ratio of assets against loans. It is interesting to note that the submission of a business plan is not a requirement for DBM lending. Although this policy reduces the exposure of the bank to risk, it opposes the stated objective of the bank: to support the SME sector and in particular to encourage entrepreneurship. Most entrepreneurs do not have sufficient assets to offer as security.

[4] A discussion of trends in commercial bank interest rates to SMEs was given in Chapter 4.

The DBM recognises this problem. It acknowledges that a better approach is to lend primarily against a sound business plan, but admits that it does not have the necessary managerial skills to evaluate effectively a business plan. This is a major deficit that needs addressing urgently.

Since none of the other SME support organisations require the production of a business plan to make support available, it appears possible to set up a business in Mauritius with no planning at all.

The nature of financial support to SMEs should be extended to cover a range of alternative options, two examples are venture capital and the establishment of credit unions. In addition, the role of the industry associations can be enhanced through their direct involvement in funding their members. All of these opportunities need to be explored in greater depth.

5.3.6 Summary of Enterprise Perceptions

Table 5.7 sets out the aggregated results for all five institutions. Although the total sample of SMEs surveyed is of an adequate size for research purposes, the level of usage is generally so low that perceptions of usefulness are expressed by often only a handful of companies. Therefore caution should be taken in using the figures for comparative purposes. Bearing this in mind, the findings are interesting.

Table 5.7: Summary of User Perceptions of SME Support Services

	% Heard of	% Used	Useful
SMIDO	67	15	3.9
EPZDA	69	23	4.3
MEDIA	73	14	3.8
IVTB	65	17	4.0
DBM	68	15	4.7(a)

Note: (a) this scoring is based on the evaluation of one service only, as in Table 5.5

It is clear that these five institutions are reasonably successful in creating awareness of their support services (between 65% and 73% of our survey responded positively). However, all are significantly less successful in persuading SMEs to participate or to make use of them. The highest percentage in this category is 23% of those companies who had heard of the services actually used them, whilst the lowest is only 14%. Where SMEs do use services, perceptions of usefulness are positive, ranging (on a scale of 1 to 5) from 3.8 at the bottom end to 4.7 at the top. The take-up response is of particular concern and we recommend further exploration of the reasons for this.

5.4 Other Support Organisations

There is a host of other organisations that offer support to the SME sector in a variety of ways. These include the Mauritius Standards Board, for advice on quality and trading standards; Subex, which aims to create subcontracting links between organisations in the engineering sector; the Technology Diffusion Service, which provides foreign consultants for technology projects; the National Computer Board, which provides some support to the IT industry; the Women Entrepreneurship Unit, which was established specifically to support women running micro-enterprises; and a number of industry associations such as the Mauritius Employers' Federation and Chambers of Commerce.

Some of these organisations, such as the MSB and the TDS, have a very clear remit, yet there is little evidence co-ordination or integration into the overall infrastructure for supporting the SME sector. It is up to the small company to discover the support offered by these organisations and to determine whether the support is appropriate.

An organisation such as the National Computer Board will lack focus if it has to switch between contributing to national policy and supporting enterprises at the micro-level. The idea of developing sub-contracting linkages which underlies SUBEX is sound. However it is currently limited to engineering activities and has a variety of other problems. These are discussed in more detail in Chapter 4.

The Women Entrepreneurship Unit concentrates on the specific issues faced by women entrepreneurs at the micro-enterprise level. Yet, many large businesses had started at the micro level. How does the overall support to SMEs in Mauritius enable a company run by one-person, say, grow into to a small, medium or large enterprise? The demarcation and separation of support based on size alone may encourage the individual supporting organisations to preserve their membership base at the expense of encouraging growth.

The trade and industry associations appear to be under-performing and are under-used in the range of support offered to SMEs. There seems to be only one association, which represents the needs of small firms in Mauritius. The Small Scale Entrepreneurs' Association of Mauritius (SSEAM) puts forward the case of small firms to policy making fora: for example, the annual pre-budgetary consultations with the private sector.[5] However, SSEAM does not appear to provide training or other services to small firms. In part it lacks the requisite capabilities and finance. Strengthening SSEAM could bring valuable gains to small firms. Increasingly the literature indicates that the most effective support to SMEs can be provided from within their own representation.[6] Here, vested interests are greater, motivation is higher, thus the resource investment is more effective. Rather than governmental organisations delivering direct support to the SME, the trend is to enhance the capabilities of the voluntary sector so that they can support their own members.

---

[5] In 1998, for instance, they made a strong case about the administrative burden resulting from the introduction of VAT on small firms. Subsequently, this was removed for small firms with low turnovers.

[6] Curran and Blackburn (1994); Gibson (1997); Nadvi (1998); Schmitz (1998)

5.5 An Assessment of the SME Support System

Our observations indicate that Mauritius is particularly well-endowed with institutions and organisations dedicated to supporting industry in general and SMEs in particular. In individual institutions, there is evidence of many positive initiatives. SMIDO is under new and energetic management with staff committed to fostering the cause of small business. Now it has its own building in a well-established industrial area. It has a renewed mandate to service SMEs and is backed by a major grant increase from central government. It is beginning to work more proactively with other SME agencies (e.g MEDIA and IVTB) to deliver its services. Within the textile industry, EPZDA has a good track-record of expertise and knowledge. It demonstrates an innovative approach to SME support, especially in relation to its use of the internet to create a forum for the diffusion and exchange of industry information. EPZDA has established the Clothing Technology Centre to provide SMEs with the opportunity of enhancing their technical skills. IVTB has a good reputation for the provision of training and related activities. It too is under new management and occupies a new building. Of all the SME support institutions, the Development Bank of Mauritius has been in operation the longest and has the potential to make one of the most significant financial contributions to SME development.

However, at the level of the support system as a whole we detect some significant deficiencies:

Lack of a strategic perspective – No single organisation has responsibility for, strategic issues relating to the whole SME sector. Thus, opportunities represented by the development of industry clusters, the encouragement of upstream and downstream linkages, and the role of indirect exporters remain unexploited. Similarly, there is no mechanism for co-ordinating governmental SME support provision or for activating an exchange between the public and private sector support frameworks.

Lack of co-ordination – The diversity of institutions and their relative autonomy contribute to a duplication of service. For example, training courses useful to the textile industry are provided by both EPZDA and IVTB. At the same time, gaps exist in the provision to specific sectors: for example, services, the IT industry and emerging industries.

An insufficient commercial approach – Institutions should be made more accountable for their activities to maximise their effectiveness. Among other things this requires:

- identifying clear visions, missions and objectives for each supporting organisation;
- establishing explicit performance indicators and transparent means of measuring performance;
- perceiving SMEs as clients rather than beneficiaries;
- enhancing the organisations' managerial and business skills. Currently, there

is insufficient understanding of industry and market dynamics, the influences on and processes of SME growth, the specific conditions within export markets, and the role and practice of strategic marketing in developing and expanding small businesses.

Lack of targeting – Service offers should become more demand-led, yet be proactively directed towards those enterprises that can best use them. Resources are allocated on a first-come, first-served basis to SMEs that request assistance, rather than to those exhibiting the greatest potential for growth. The World Bank estimate[7] a cost of US$4,250 to create one job in a small firm, through enterprise development interventions. Given limited and diminishing resources, it should be decided which companies should be supported and how this is to be achieved.

Lack of direction – There is an assumption that, as long as SMEs are offered a menu of support activities, they are able to identify the help they need. This thinking is inherently defective. Inexperienced entrepreneurs cannot know the precise nature of the most effective support: just as a sick patient is unlikely to know the best treatment for his or her disease. It is the doctor's job, or in this case an SME consultant, to advise the small business of the range of "treatments", taking into account the nature of the firm and its industrial context.

Lack of diversity in approaches to interventions – Training is properly recognised as a useful intervention, yet there is a tendency to view it as a panacea. Unfortunately many training courses are too generic and academic to provide fast-track support needed by SMEs. Alternative and innovative styles of support is not fully exploited.

Lack of engagement with the private sector – Insufficient demand is made of the private sector, particularly trade associations and private training and information providers.

5.6 Conclusions

These preliminary findings provide valuable insights into the nature and coverage of the public sector SME institutional system Mauritius. Undoubtedly, the investment in SME support is not delivering the growth required or expected at the enterprise level and this must be improved. An overhaul of the entire SME support system is required to address the deficiencies outlined above, and to create a more cohesive integrated framework. The strategies we are proposing in Chapter 6 aim to deliver a much more focused, targeted and client-driven approach to SME support.

---

[7] Manu (1998)

6 Proposals for SME Competitiveness

6.1 Introduction

This chapter draws on the findings of previous chapters and presents a menu of recommendations to enhance the competitiveness of small firms in Mauritius. It is hoped that our suggestions will achieve three basic objectives:

(a) Remove policy and institutional impediments to direct SME exporting;

(b) Reduce policy and institutional obstacles to indirect exporting from SMEs i.e., sub-contracting/supplier relations between SMEs and large export firms.

(c) Provide ideas on new products and activities that can be undertaken by SMEs in both the domestic and export market.

Although our fieldwork was restricted to three activities (textiles, printing and publishing, and information technology), the suggestions are applicable to most small firms in the Mauritian manufacturing and service sectors. The suggestions are grouped under several headings: macroeconomic policies, trade policies, bureaucratic procedures, finance, technological support, clusters and linkages, human capital, private sector initiatives, data collection and monitoring of SME performance, new areas for SMEs. The chapter should be read in conjunction with the policy table given in the executive summary. The policy table shows a possible sequencing of the recommendations, highlighting those that are most appropriate in the short-term (defined as one year) and the medium-term (four years). It also gives guidance on possible implementing agencies for each idea. Further work needs to be done in Mauritius to refine and put these proposals into operation.

6.2 Macroeconomic Policies

The objective is to ensure a stable macroeconomic climate with low inflation and reasonable economic growth to foster SME and overall private sector investment. The main recommendations to achieve this are as follows:

- Develop a plan to reduce the budget deficit by 25% through civil service and public enterprise reform within three years. Less crowding out by the public sector, along with more private investment and growth, will create further opportunities for small firms.

- Persist with a stable, slightly depreciated real exchange rate to encourage exports from SMEs. Budget deficit reduction – which will reduce inflationary pressures – will assist in real exchange rate management. Continue with monitoring cross-country behaviour in real exchange rate management so that local firms are not disadvantaged in export markets *vis-à-vis* international competitors.

- The restoration of low, stable interest rates for large and small firms is also dependent on deficit reduction, backed by prudent monetary policy.

6.3 Trade Policies

6.3.1 Import Liberalisation

The objective is to achieve a low and uniform level of effective protection for manufacturing of about 15% within 4 years. Increased competition from imports will provide incentives for SMEs to restructure, upgrade and move into exports. The main recommendations to achieve this are as follows:

- Reactivate the programme of import liberalisation. Set specific advance targets for phased reductions in import tariffs. This will give small and large firms strong signals to restructure.

- Phase out protection for highly protected activities that lack clear economic rationale such as clothing, food, footwear and furniture. These four sectors have large SME populations and would benefit from the spur of international competition. These activities can become future exports within a relatively short period with focussed technological and human capital assistance to promote productivity and quality improvement.

- Entrust the task of import liberalisation to a small, powerful tariff reform committee (e.g. 3-4 persons), which should draw up a simple, clear programme for tariff reform and monitor implementation. This committee should be supported by an international economics consultancy firm with a track record in trade policy reform. The tariff reform committee should have a limited life (e.g. 4 years) and be disbanded after completion of the achievement of the 15% effective rate of protection.

6.3.2 Export Promotion

The objective is to strengthen the export promotion system and to offset the anti-export bias of the trade regime facing some direct and indirect SME exporters. The main recommendations to achieve this are as follows:

- Ensure quick and easy access to duty-free imported inputs for direct and indirect SME exporters. The systems for granting EPZ certificates and duty-drawback rebates, for instance, should be further streamlined and accelerated by using paperless email communication between the relevant authorities and firms as well as introducing strict processing times of a maximum of three days. Possible abuses of these systems could be regulated by random checks and heavy fines rather than screening every application.
- Develop realistic raw material wastage provision/ratios for all potential export sectors to permit sub-contracting between large firms and SMEs.
- Consolidate export promotion activities, currently based in Mauritius, into a major promotion event, Mauritius Week. An outline of this is shown in Appendix 4 Box 1.
- Establish a network of shops throughout Mauritius for tourists as joint ventures between the government and business associations. This idea is shown in Appendix 4, Box 2. These should function along commercial lines with an agenda for full privatisation. Internationally competitive SMEs and indirect SME exporters should be encouraged to sell through these shops. Where their output does not meet international quality standards, the requisite technical support should be given to them by the Business Link (see Appendix 4, Box 4).
- Strengthen MEDIA's overseas presence by establishing trade promotion offices in key markets (see Appendix 4, Box 3). These should function independently of overseas embassies, should be adequately funded and staffed by marketing professionals. These offices should give equal weight to promoting exports from large firms and SMEs. They could be established as joint ventures between the government and business associations (with a time-bound agenda for full privatisation). To start with, one office might be in the UK for Europe, one in the US for North America and Canada and one in a suitable location for Africa.
- MEDIA to establish a dedicated web site for SME exporters on a user cost basis. Eventually the running of this could be transferred to the proposed Federation of SME associations (see Section 6.9 below).

6.4 Bureaucratic Procedures

The objective is to reduce significantly the transactions cost to business caused by the administrative procedures of the public sector. The main recommendations to achieve this are as follows:
- Radically streamline the administrative procedures on business start-up which currently impede SME development. Two areas are particularly important:

- ✓ *Local government permits*: (a) Merge Development/Building/Local Authority permits into one permit issued by one organisation. Set a maximum time limit for administrating this permit (e.g. two weeks). (b) Eliminate the need for start-up clearances from the police, fire services, Ministry of the Environment, Factory inspectorate and Ministry of Health. (c) Provide clear guidelines on all health, safety, security issues to new businesses and a helpline for advice on compliance. Carry out inspections on a random basis or on the basis of specific complaints.

- ✓ *Work/residence permits*: (a) Centralise all work/residence permit approvals in the Passport and Immigration Office and considerably speed up processing times. (b) Dispense with approval from the Prime Ministers Office and the Ministry of Education and Human Resource Development for work/residence permits. (c) Grant automatic 3 year work permits for expatriate managers and high-level technical staff upon FDI approval. (d) Allow firms to extend work permits for expatriate managers and high-level technical staff automatically for 3 years upon payment of an appropriate fee.

- Implement the proposal for the Board of Investment to streamline radically the approval procedures for FDI and joint ventures between foreign firms and local SMEs. The new FDI will generate sub-contracting and supplier relations for SMEs with the requisite manufacturing capabilities.

- Commission a comprehensive red tape analysis of the impact of administrative procedures on SME start-up and operations (e.g. tax processes, obtaining title to land and premises, Ministry of Labour approvals, customs registration, other approvals etc). The results of the analysis should be implemented within one year. Target administrative steps that can be removed with low political costs, or without changes to existing laws. Then reform existing laws to reduce procedures.

- Set clear and uniform guidelines for all administrative procedures affecting the private sector. Monitor administrative processing standards (particularly for those regulations affecting SMEs) and publicise the results.

6.5 Finance

The twin objectives are to improve access to finance for SMEs and to reduce real interest rates for SME lending. The main recommendations are as follows:

- Implement the proposals for a Mutual Guarantee Fund and a Venture Capital Fund.

- Privatise the management of the Development Bank of Mauritius. Wholesale privatisation is sometimes considered an option for development banks. The difficulty with this is that a privatised DBM might lack sufficient commitment to social goals: such as, SMEs preferring to focus on more profitable types of lending and financial operations. This may not be feasible politically. Significant efficiency gains can be realised by bringing in aggressive private managers and allowing the DBM to operate as if a private firm even if ownership of assets is not transferred. A management contract, whereby the government pays a private firm a fee for managing the DBM, might be an acceptable option. It avoids the risk of asset concentration in the banking sector, can improve productivity and can radically streamline bureaucracy. The best form of contract is a fee-for-service arrangement coupled with the incentive to improve efficiency and profitability. Its performance should be carefully monitored by the Bank of Mauritius.

- Establish an Export Development Fund by hiving off the industrial estates of MEDIA and DBM to the private sector to create an export development fund for SMEs marketing efforts. Amongst other things, this fund could subsidise costs of participating in foreign trade fairs, contact promotion programmes, marketing studies and web sites for individual SMEs. Large business houses in Mauritius already run industrial estates and the private sector could profitably expand in this direction. The Export Development Fund can be topped up by some of the proceeds from future privatisation of state-owned enterprises.

- Foster the creation of credit unions in SME associations. At its basic level, this is an arrangement where members pay in a set amount on a regular basis. They can draw out up to the amount they have put in. It is akin to a forced savings scheme. If each of the 5731 manufacturing SMEs contributes $1000, this will generate over $5.7 million worth of new capital. In the next stage of development the credit union invests the money and allows SMEs to borrow more than they put in.

6.6 Technological Support

6.6.1. Establish a Business Link

The objective is to provide a targeted, tailored and directive infrastructure for delivering assistance to SMEs from start-up to the level of growth that takes the enterprise out of the SME definition.

The Business Link is a co-ordinating mechanism to harness and allocate the full range of required support inputs to SMEs from both the public and private sectors. It would replace all existing governmental or parastatal organisations supporting SMEs at the enterprise level. Details of the Business Link concept, adapted from the model established and operating effectively in the UK, are described in Appendix 4, Box 4.

We would propose that, if the concept of a Business Link is accepted in principle, then the Chief Executive of a Business Link in the UK should act as a consultant for its development and implementation in Mauritius.

6.6.2 Design House

The objective is to enhance design skills in SMEs and to strengthen a design culture in Mauritius.

It is widely acknowledged that Mauritius needs design skills to add value in the textile industry, as well as in other manufacturing and service activities. Although there has been an increase in the range of design education courses, this is a slow way to build commercially viable design capability. The Design House offers a speedier and more effective alternative. A detailed explanation is provided in Appendix 4, Box 5.

6.6.3 Textile Council

The objective is to create a dedicated support institution for the textile sector. The main recommendation to achieve this is to reformulate EPZDA as a Textile Council. It would act primarily as an advisory, knowledge-building and policy-making body on all issues related to the textile and garment production industry. It would pass direct involvement with SME and enterprise development to the Business Link, which would work together with a newly-formed Textile Industry Association.

In accordance with this positioning, we envisage that the Textile Council would retain service offers such as the Trend Forum, the Industry Focus publication, its information services and the Clothing Technology Centre. It would relinquish its consultancy and training services. Activities of the User Group, such as seminars on textile issues, would become open fora. New initiatives are likely to flow from this. Two simple ideas for the further development of the Clothing Technology Centre as a resource are shown in Appendix 4, Box 6.

6.7 Clusters and Linkages

The objective is to foster the creation of industrial clusters and intra-firm networks. The underpinning concepts supporting this initiative are outlined in Appendix 4, Box 7. The main recommendations to achieve this are as follows:

- Merge SUBEX-M within SMIDO. This would involve little restructuring and transaction cost as SUBEX-M is already housed in the SMIDO building in Mauritius. However, the change would properly institutionalise, fund and sustain the country's only intra-firm linkage programme, focussed on engineering.

- Develop a new programme to upgrade suppliers in textiles, clothing and food products. The more focussed linkage programme for these three light industries should be built on existing marketing chains with foreign buyers. Small firms in an existing marketing relationship would have benefited from cumulative learning and indirect exporting to foreign markets. The programme should also have a strong private sector orientation and draw on inputs from public technology institutions (such as the Mauritius Bureau of Standards) and soft loan windows of the commercialised DBM. The public sector aspect of the new programme could be jointly co-ordinated by SMIDO and MEDIA. The latter has direct contact with international buyers and knowledge of the price, quality and delivery requirements of international markets while the former is familiar with the capabilities of the SME population.

6.8 Human Capital

The objective is to enhance human resources at the individual and the organisational level. The following recommendations are made:

- Cost effective reduction of absenteeism through national campaigns. An example might be called "Don't Miss Monday" and could involve the use of roadside posters, leaflets distributed at the workplace, a national competition and television coverage.
- Upgrade vocational capabilities by increasing certification and tailoring training more closely to the needs of industry. It is proposed that IVTB take the following action:
  - ✓ *Refocus on core business*: Concentrate on designing and delivering academically validated vocational education and training courses in close collaboration with industry and industry associations.
  - ✓ *Short courses*: Drop non-validated short courses and pass these to the private sector. IVTB should be responsible for monitoring the quality of private sector training and institute an "IVTB Seal of Approval" scheme for approved private sector courses.
- Identify and reduce skill and educational gaps in potential areas of comparative advantage. This can be done in a number of ways:
  - ✓ *Sandwich courses*: Expand the range of university degree courses that incorporate a work placement in order to give students greater exposure and hands-on experience of industry. Encourage students to find work placements overseas.
  - ✓ *Scholarships*: Provide more scholarships for students to study abroad.

Allocation of this investment should be based on the identification of strategically important skill gaps (e.g. information technology, business studies and engineering activities).

✓ *Mauritian returnees*: Create incentives to encourage Mauritian professionals to return from overseas. Support should focus on attracting skills in key areas, such as information technology, business studies and engineering activities.

6.9 Private Sector Initiatives

The objectives under this heading are to strengthen significantly SME associations as well as the relationship between SMEs, the Business Link and the commercial banks. The main recommendations to achieve these objectives are as follows:

- The SMEs themselves should establish individual industrial associations for key sectors. The Small Scale Entrepreneur Association of Mauritius (SSEAM) should be re-positioned as a federation of individual SME associations. The new Federation should be the principal advocate for SMEs in Mauritius, liase with government bodies, and deliver centralised generic services to its members (e.g. an information/resource centre for SMEs). It should also become a full member of the Joint Economic Council and continue to participate in policy consultations such as the pre-budget consultations. The sector-specific industrial associations should represent their members' interests and provide selected common services (e.g. run a credit union for members and bulk-buy raw materials and equipment). These associations should be properly funded and run professionally by their members.

- The private sector (including SMEs) should actively support service delivery by the Business Link. Actions might include: providing consultants, advice on future services, and providing feedback on services.

- To assist SMEs in the strategic and practical aspects of exporting, the development of a new industry sub-sector of export houses and export consultancies should be encouraged. These organisations would support the Business Link as well as acting as an additional independent resource for SMEs. A detailed explanation of this concept is given in Appendix 4, Box 8.

- Commercial banks should strengthen their relations with SMEs. Actions might include: appointing specialist small business advisors, training staff to better understand SME financial needs and researching SME issues and disseminating this to clients.

- Business associations and large firms could assist considerably with skill development for small firms by providing more short in-plant placements for university students and launching training centres/schemes for middle management, production management and designers.

6.10 Data Collection & Monitoring of SME Performance

The objectives are to develop a consistent definition of SMEs and to monitor SME performance. The main recommendations to achieve this are:

- Formulate a more inclusive definition of the SME sector: for example one that includes the service sector; acknowledges that the value of capital investment no longer necessarily represents a source of competitive advantage and that advantage is shifting towards the value of human capital; and recognises that the smallest possible enterprise, i.e. the microenterprise, has the potential to evolve into a much larger organisation. For simplicity, an SME could be a manufacturing firm with less than 50 employees, or a services firm with less than 20 employees. In both cases, they should be firms that are independent and not subsidiaries of a larger organisation (see Chapter 1).

- Create a database on SME performance. This will involve developing key SME performance indicators and an annual survey of SME perceptions of the policy environment and the quality of institutional support. The results of these surveys should inform future policy-making on SMEs. Enterprise viewpoints on new policy suggestions could be tested using the annual survey of policies and institutions. The survey could be supplemented by regular focal group discussions between senior public officials and representative SMEs.

6.11 New Areas for SMEs

Throughout this report, we have emphasised repeatedly that the smaller company cannot hope to compete against its larger competitors in terms of scale. Nonetheless a strategic advantage can be created and sustained by combining: a careful market selection strategy; the design and delivery of high value-added, differentiated products and services; and (where appropriate) collaboration with market leaders in the form of long-term trading contracts, strategic alliances or joint ventures.

Quite simply the challenge for SMEs in Mauritius is to determine the products or services that should be offered to specific markets. Successful strategies will be specialised, will exploit national or firm-specific advantages and probably will involve a high degree of interpersonal involvement and relationship-building.

In addition, significant opportunities exist for Mauritius to leverage its success in achieving levels of economic growth substantially higher than its African neighbours by offering consultancy services to other African countries. Proposals contained in this chapter for the development of private sector export houses and marketing consultancies are not only designed to enhance the export competitiveness of Mauritian firms, but also to represent an export opportunity.

Whilst, undoubtedly, Mauritius needs a general diversification of its commercial base, this study is concerned with only three specific industry sectors. Possible future directions for SMEs in the sectors examined in this report are:

Table 6.1   New Areas for SMES in Textiles, Printing and IT

Industry sector	Products/services	Markets
Textiles	Swimwear	OECD
	Lingerie	OECD
	Specialist sportswear, e.g. for scuba diving sailing, climbing	OECD
	Design and technical services	Africa and other developing countries
Printing and publishing	Copy shops (see Kall Kwik)	Domestic
	Pre-press	OECD
	Design	Africa and other developing countries
	Electronic media, e.g. CD-Rom, internet, intranet	Africa and other developing countries
IT	Internet cafés	Domestic
	System integration services, e.g. computerised banking systems	OECD investment in Africa
	IT support, e.g. helpdesks	Africa and other developing countries
	Call centres	OECD

APPENDIX 1

The Enterprise Survey

The objectives of the empirical research of SMEs are to highlight the technological, marketing and human capital capabilities of Mauritian enterprises; to analyse the influence of the policy regime on small firm competitiveness; and to examine the adequacy of institutional support for small firms.

Three industries were selected in order to identify both the issues common to all SMEs and those specific to a sector. The choice of industries, textiles, printing/publishing and IT, was made on the basis of suggestions for strategically-important industries contained in Lall and Wignaraja (1998).

SMIDO arranged appointments with up to twenty of their members, spread across these three sectors. Semi-structured interviews of between one hour and three hours were held with nineteen companies, followed (where appropriate) by a visit to the factory or offices. Four companies had more than the 100 employees specified as the maximum for the SME sector. Three were included for the following reasons:

L'inattendu Ltd – A woman-headed firm, and also as an example of good management practices. Aline Wong, the entrepreneur, has won a prize in the US for being a successful female business manager, and is well known in Mauritius for the achievements of her business.

Beachwear Export Ltd – A company specialising in a high-value, niche product group (swimwear). High-value, niche products offer small companies in Mauritius more favourable opportunities for entering and succeeding in export markets.

Bowman International Sports Ltd – A call centre operation. This use of IT, leveraging the bi-lingual capabilities of Mauritians, presents a much larger opportunity for the exporting of IT services. The interview suggested that the value of exports is extremely large placing this company outside the SME sector.

Self-completion questionnaires were sent to all the interviewees plus an additional 31 companies, also spread across the three sectors, making a total of 50. Twenty-five responses to the questionnaire were received. The table below shows the composition of the total sample of 34 companies researched.

Table A.1: Composition of Sample Survey

Industry sector/Company	Main product	Value of exports (1997 $US)	No. of employees
Textiles			
Beachwear Export Ltd	Swimwear	N/A	125
Exotic Design	T-shirts and casualwear	48,309	120
Fleur de Lys	Lingerie	Not exporting	15
G&T Action Wear Ltd	T-shirts, shorts	N/A	45
Island Style	T-shirts, shorts	170,240	35
La Chance Ltd	T-shirts, shorts	538,164	98
L'inattendu Ltd	Ladies jersey casualwear, children's wear	1,410500	130
Maraly Fashion	Lingerie	Not exporting	15
Meem Ltd	Baby and children's wear	4,865	7
Metro-Garments Manufacturing Ltd	School uniforms, shirts, T-shirts	53,500	20
Nancy Garment Ltd	T-shirts	Not exporting	40
Nobee Ltd	Children's wear, ladies wear	4,860	10
M R Rambarran Brothers	T-shirts	Not exporting	6
Mr D Ramgoolam & Sons	Uniforms, tailored suits for men and women	Not exporting	5
Tamak Ltd	Jersey garments	Not exporting	N/A
Woven Labels (Mauritius) Ltd	Woven labels + printed suits for men and women	N/A	300
Zubda Co Ltd	Babywear	Not exporting	6
Printing and publishing			
Arsenius Printing and Stationery Ltd	Books, general stationery	Not exporting	5
Badat Printing	General stationery	Not exporting	2
BL Cataland	Pre-press and pre-media	2,918,140	20
Compocenter	Pre-press	583,640	40
Cosmoprint Co Ltd	Corporate stationery	Not exporting	10
De Luxe Printing	General stationery	Not exporting	23
Kalligraphia Ltd	Corporate stationery, point of sale material, packaging	Not exporting	9
MediaDesign Ltd	CD-Roms	Not exporting	5
Nu-print Ltd	Printed materials for the textile industry	7,287	21
Précigraph Ltd	Books and corporate stationery	424,130	70
Quad Printers	Corporate stationery	1,952	16
St Francois Printing Co Ltd	General stationery	Not exporting	5

Industry sector/Company	Main product	Value of exports, 1997 $US	No. of employees
IT			
Babic Co Ltd	Computer hardware	252,901	11
Bowman International Sports Ltd	Call centre	N/A	210
D&H Computer Services	Software development	Not trading	6
London Information Systems Ltd	Photocopier consumables, IT services	N/A	22
Mauritius Computing Services	Software for the sugar industry	Not exporting	29

Industry sector – Of the 34 firms researched, 17 are in the garment manufacture business, reflecting the general distribution of SMEs. Twelve firms are in the printing and publishing sector, and five are engaged in various information technology activities.

Main product – Ten of the thirteen firms in garment manufacture produce casualwear, predominantly from cotton weave and cotton jersey. Two specialise in baby and childrenswear, and the others in swimwear, lingerie, woven labels, uniforms and tailoring.

Of the printing and publishing companies, eight produce corporate and general stationery, i.e. annual reports, brochures, posters, letterheads, etc, one specialises in labels and tags for the clothing industry, two are in pre-press and pre-media, and one produces CD-Roms.

Within IT, one company is solely involved in the sale of computer hardware. Another has three areas of activity: the sale of computer hardware, the sale of photocopier consumables and IT services. Yet another operates as a call centre, taking sporting bets from the US, another compnay develops software for the sugar industry, and one acts purely as a production department of a UK company, upgrading software for the steel industry.

Value of exports for 1997 in $US – In our sample, figures were available for 14 companies. These range from nearly $3 million to as low as $1,952. Fifteen companies do not export and one company is not trading at all.

Number of employees – With over 100 staff, five enterprises should be categorised as large firms. Nine are micro-enterprises with less than 10 employees. Two could be classified as a medium-size enterprises, one with 98 employees and the other with 70, and the remainder fall into the category of small enterprises, with employees numbering from 10 to 45.

The graph below shows the export destinations of the sample.

Figure A.1: Number of Companies Exporting and Their Destinations

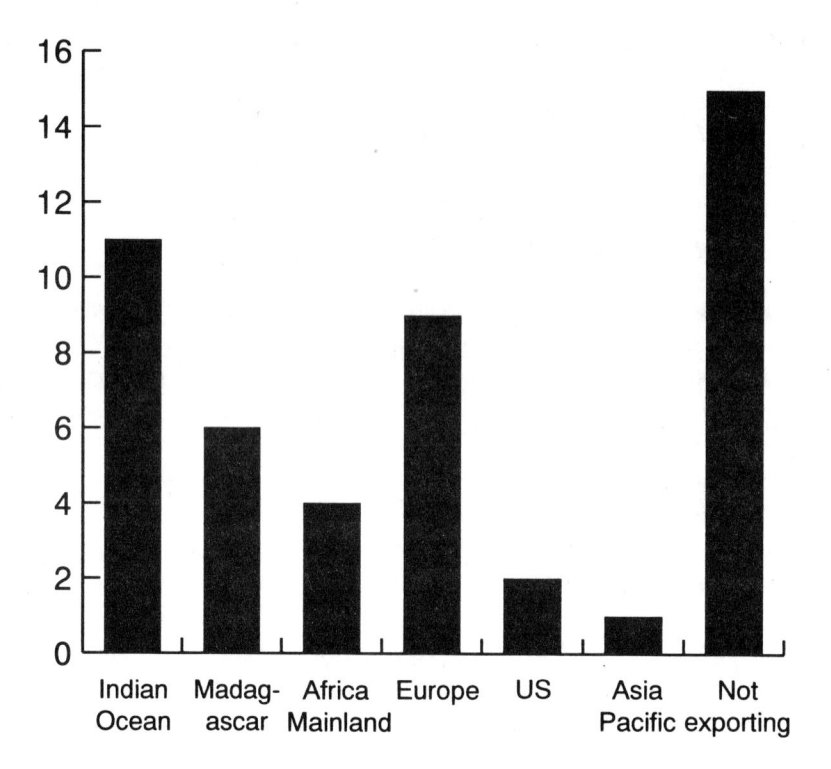

Destination	Number
Indian Ocean	11
Madagascar	6
Africa Mainland	4
Europe	9
US	2
Asia Pacific	1
Not exporting	15

APPENDIX 2

A Framework for Evaluating SME Capabilities

Any firm, whether large or small, exists as part of a broader infrastructure, a macro-environment that is shaped by the impact of global trade, national policies, industry structures and sources of competitive advantage, the availability of and access to resources, and competitor activity. The way in which an individual enterprise responds to these macro-environmental influences the nature and degree of its performance.

Performance can be measured in many ways. Volume of sales, profitability, return on investment, market share are just some of the quantifiable measures that can be an organisation's commercial objectives. For the purposes of this study, and as a reflection of the principle imperative for national economic growth in developing countries, we have chosen export performance as the key focus, and the value of exports as its simple measure.

A successful growth process, in this case towards exporting, involves the enterprise in capitalising on external opportunities and implementing appropriate and timely responses or changes in the firm's internal organisation. This process depends on: (i) the growth or export-orientation of the owner-manager (driven by his or her managerial characteristics); (ii) the strategy pursued; and (iii) the competences (within the enterprise) that can be employed to implement strategic decisions. The figure below illustrates how these three factors contribute to the export performance of SMEs at the level of the enterprise. This framework is adapted from research by Chetty and Hamilton (1996), and builds on a number of other studies on the determinants and influences of export performance and behaviour, particularly in the SME sector.[1]

Strategy

Strategy is defined as the decisions made by the firm as to the products that are sold to which markets and how the company leverages competitive advantage, i.e. the benefits delivered to customers that are distinctive and differentiated from their competitors.

Market selection – Unlike larger companies, the SME lacks the scale and resources to compete on an industry-wide basis, producing many products or services and selling to a diversity of markets. A niche strategy, as suggested by Porter (1980) (and supported by numerous studies on SMEs[2]), offers the best route to sustainable performance. Here, the

---

[1] For example, Philp (1998), Aaby and Slater (1989), Bilkey and Tesar (1997), Louter et al. (1991).
[2] See Barber et al (1992); Hall (1995) for quantitative research confirming the link between performance and a focus or niche strategy. See also Gantisky (1989) for examples of the implementation of niche strategies by SMEs in a small country.

firm focuses on a narrow range of products or services targeted at one or a limited number of customer markets. In order to make sound decisions on market selection, the enterprise must have information about future or existing markets. It has to evaluate the potential of these markets and assess the strategic fit between market and the firm's ability to meet those needs.

Figure A.2: Enterprise Dynamics and Exporting

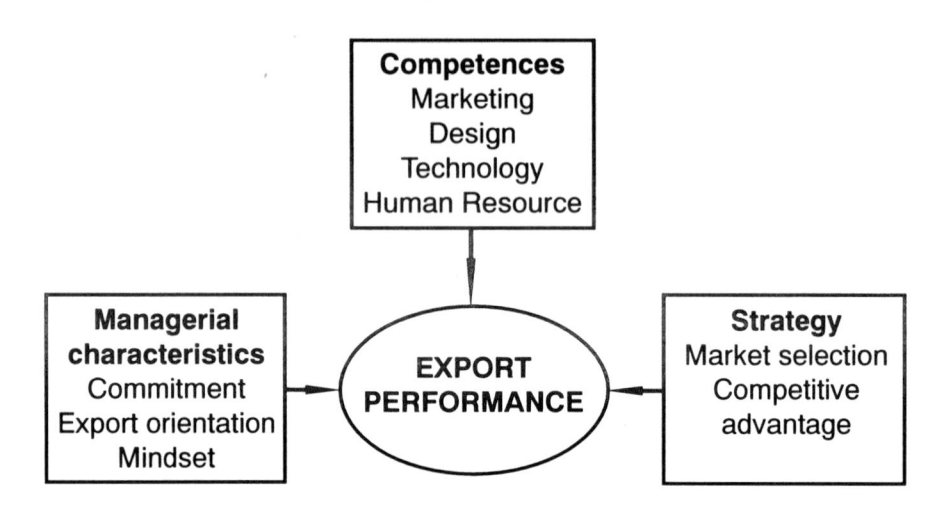

```
                    ┌──────────────────┐
                    │   Competences    │
                    │    Marketing     │
                    │      Design      │
                    │    Technology    │
                    │  Human Resource  │
                    └────────┬─────────┘
                             │
                             ▼
┌──────────────────┐   ┌───────────┐   ┌──────────────────┐
│   Managerial     │   │           │   │    Strategy      │
│ characteristics  │   │  EXPORT   │   │ Market selection │
│   Commitment     │──▶│PERFORMANCE│◀──│   Competitive    │
│ Export orientation│  │           │   │    advantage     │
│     Mindset      │   └───────────┘   └──────────────────┘
└──────────────────┘
```

Competitive advantage – The firm must choose the basis on which it aims to compete. For example, establishing its position on the price-quality spectrum, taking into account the benefits to customers and the offers made by competitors. The package of benefits provided is termed its 'proposition' and this needs to be differentiated from the competition in a way that is perceived by customers as delivering value. Sources of competitive advantage are numerous. The SME, pursuing a niche or focus strategy, might include unique high-quality products, fast delivery, a propensity to innovate, or close relationships with customers or distributors.

Competences

Competences are defined as the capabilities at the functional level of an enterprise that are used to implement strategy. In most cases, competences relate to the functional areas of a business: marketing, production and the use of technology, human resource and finance. They also include support activities such as research and development and design. For the purposes of this study, we have chosen to examine SMEs in terms of their competences in marketing, design, the use of technology, and human resource.

Marketing – Marketing capabilities are the way the firm uses the tools of the marketing mix to deliver competitive advantage. These tools relate to decisions on product – what products or services are produced and with what characteristics; price – the level at which prices are set and how prices may be varied; distribution – how products or services are made accessible to customers; and promotion – how customers are made aware of products and services.

Design – Design has an important role to play in delivering competitive advantage by making tangible the needs and aspirations of customers. For example, fashion design in the garment manufacturing business, creates clothing that the target customers will find more appealing than that of competitors. Graphic design creates promotional material to communicate with and persuade the target market. Interior design can create a physical environment that supports a high quality retail outlet. The way that organisations use design skills and manage design projects is a competence that is increasingly identified as a major source of competitive advantage.

Technology – A firm's choice of position on the price-quality spectrum, or any other basis on which it chooses to compete, is facilitated by the use of appropriate and up-to-date technology. However, in many industries, the nature of the technology employed is increasingly shifting emphasis from capital equipment for production towards the effective use of information and processes. Technological competence is the way the firm uses all aspects of technology to deliver competitive advantage.

Human resources – There is a growing recognition that any organisation's single, most valuable resource any organisation has is its people. Strategic decisions are made and implemented by people; functional capabilities are realised by people. The performance of individuals is a function of their own personality, their skills and training, their motivation and the organisational culture of the workplace. The firm's ability to attract, retain and nurture its people is a key competence.

Managerial characteristics

The characteristics of senior staff, in particular the owner-manager, underpin the firm's growth or export-orientation and define its strategic choices and the way it develops and uses key competences. These "soft" factors are increasingly viewed as critically important for the SME, where the influence of the owner-manager is paramount.[3] Additionally, identification of the managerial characteristics that are most conducive to pursuing export targets can help the SME allocate the appropriate resources services. We have considered three characteristics: commitment to growth, export orientation, and a global or international mindset.

Commitment to growth – Not all small businesses aim for growth. Those that do, will benefit most from assistance from external sources. The identification of a growth

---

[3] Philp (1998); Jennings and Beaver (1997); Moran (1998); Srinivas (1995).

orientation should be a major criterion for the allocation of resources offered by business development services.

Export orientation – Similarly, not all small businesses are interested in exporting. Those that are, make a conscious decision to allocate scarce internal resources to exploiting export opportunities and to bear additional risk.

A *global or international* mindset – Where an owner-manager has a personal outward orientation and, often, direct exposure to international influences, the greater his or her propensity to engage successfully in exporting.

APPENDIX 3

Permits/Clearances Required for Setting Up of an Enterprise

Before starting their operations, industrialists are required to obtain a number of administrative permits. The following is a list of main permits/clearances required for establishing an enterprise.

Development/Building Permit

i. A development permit for construction purposes from the Local Authority concerned (i.e. Municipalities in urban areas and District Councils in rural areas) where the construction of a building to accommodate the factory is envisaged. A building permit is also required from the Municipality in urban areas and from the Ministry of Works in rural areas.

ii. A permit for the running of a business from the Local Authority (Municipality or District Council).

Permit from Local Authority

Before the issue of permit at (ii), clearance from the following Ministries/Departments is required by the Local Authority:

a) Ministry of Health, Regional Public Health Office (Sanitary Issues)

b) Ministry of Environment, 9th Floor, Ken Lee Tower, Cr. St. Georges and Barracks Streets, Port Louis (Environmental Impact Assessment)

c) Factory Inspectorate, Ministry of Labour and Industrial Relations, 16 Dr. Eugene Laurent Street, Port Louis (Health and Safety)

d) Fire Services, Cr. St. Georges and De Poivre Streets, Port Louis (Fire Security)

e) Police Department (District Headquarters) (Police Security) Relevant information and documents should be submitted to these Ministries/Departments

Electric Motor Permit

iii. An Electric Motor Permit from the Ministry of Public Infrastructure, is necessary when the factory is located in rural areas.

Application for Foreign Investment

iv. Application for foreign investment in respect of foreign investors should be made to the Prime

		Minister's Office. Funds can be transferred only after Letter of Intent is issued by the Prime Minister's Office. After the funds are transferred, that Office issues the certificate of Authority which allows the non-citizen to acquire shares in Mauritius.
Work Permit	v.	Application for Work permits in respect of expatriate staff, including foreign investors to the Ministry of Education and Human Resource development, 10th Floor, Sterling House, Lislet Geoffroy Street, Port Louis.
Residence Permit	vi.	Application for residence permit from the Passport and Immigration Office, Line Barracks, Port Louis, in respect of expatriate staff, including the foreign investors.
Water Supply	vii.	Application for water supply to the Central Authority, Royal Road, Phoenix.
Electricity Supply	viii.	Application for electricity supply to the Central Electricity Board, Royal Road, Curepipe.
Telephone and Telefax Services	ix.	Application for telefax and telephone services to the Mauritius Telecom, Telecom Tower, Edity Cavell Street, Port Louis.
National Pension Fund	x.	Registration as an employer at the Ministry of Social Security for contribution to the National Pension Fund in favour of their employees.

Application forms in respect of (iv) and (v) above are available at the One Stop Shop.

Source: Ministry of Industry and Commerce (1998)

APPENDIX 4

Profiles of Selected Institutions and Policies for SMEs

> **Box 1 – Mauritius Week: Carnival in the Indian Ocean**
>
> MEDIA organises a range of promotional activities in Mauritius itself, but these are dispersed throughout the calendar year. As a result, they lack focus and profile and are expensive to promote on an individual basis. Mauritius Week would consolidate all of MEDIA's island-based promotion into one extremely high profile "extravaganza".
>
> Mauritius Week would be a week-long series of activities and events running simultaneously in a number of locations across the island. Its objectives would be to:
>
> - Promote Mauritius as a desirable location for foreign investors;
> - Promote Mauritius as a desirable tourist destination;
> - Promote Mauritius as a world-class conference centre;
> - Showcase Mauritian culture and achievements – art and craft, music, dance, drama, education, trade, innovation, etc;
> - Celebrate the "joy" of Mauritius.
>
> As such, Mauritius Week would target overseas investors, tourists, trading partners, and cultural partners. It would also serve as a focus for Mauritians themselves to acknowledge, promote, work towards and celebrate their own achievements.
>
> Appropriate events and activities are numerous, but might include:
> - The existing MITEX and buyer/seller meets
> - Trade fairs specifically for the SME sector
> - Conferences, seminars and workshops on a range of topics and subjects
> - Open days at key institutions, such as the University, or the Clothing Technology Centre
> - Organised visits to model factories, farms, etc

- Nature trails and outdoor activities and competitions
- A fashion show

Mauritius Week would raise considerable revenues during the week itself, as well as develop longer-term opportunities. Hotel prices could be raised and to supplement limited accommodation, a scheme such as "At Home in London" currently operating in London, could be implemented. Here, individual households are encouraged to make available rooms in their homes for tourists, who pay them an amount based on the quality of the accommodation. The scheme is operated by specialised agencies and householders are exempt from tax up to a certain level of income.

By focusing all of the island-based promotion into one week and extending its remit to encompass, not only trade, but also culture, Mauritius Week would have the critical mass and impetus to become a major date in the international calendar.

Box 2 – "Mauritian Soul": A showcase for Mauritian excellence

Tourists come to Mauritius with money to spend and go home with much of it in their pockets. There is virtually nothing for them to buy. They may take advantage of the cheap prices of cashmere sweaters, but they will find little of any quality to give as presents or to remind them of their holiday.

Mauritian Soul is a working title for a network of shops offering art, crafts, homeware, jewellery, fashion accessories and other products of the highest quality, all reflecting the culture of Mauritius. The shops would be located in prime positions in Port Louis and the main tourist destinations. They would have a strong brand identity, their interiors would embody good design and sophisticated merchandising, and product selection would be stringent.

It is acknowledged that these products do not exist currently in Mauritius. However, the twin forces of the Design House creating the impetus at the production end, and Mauritian Soul providing the retail outlet, will enable scores of micro-businesses to be formed or existing businesses to improve the quality of their products.

Mauritian Soul, together with the Design House, would contribute to the creation of a Mauritian style that could play a major role in all aspects of export promotion.

The Design Council will be responsible, initially, for developing and managing this initiative in order to set and maintain design and quality standards. Once established, the shops represent an opportunity for franchising.

A similar initiative has been successful in Israel.

Box 3 – Trade Promotion Offices: Getting Closer to the Customer

Trade Promotion Offices are established in key export markets for a number of purposes. To:
- Create a national presence in the export market as a focal point for inward enquiries related to importing, direct investment, etc;
- Gather data and information on environmental factors in the export market, e.g. tariffs, economic conditions, regulatory issues, etc;
- Identify and make contact with potential customers, using techniques such as direct marketing;
- Facilitate involvement in trade fairs and exhibitions, run seminars and workshops, and generally raise awareness of the value of Mauritian products and services;
- Act as a showcase for Mauritian products and services, through the use of a showroom, brochures, CD-Roms, etc.

A recent study examining the impact of Trade Promotion Offices on the exports of developing economies into OECD countries demonstrated that the presence of a TPO in a country is positively correlated with a higher share of imports coming from developing countries for product groups available from both developed and developing countries (Gabriel, Benito, Gripsrud, 1997).

For a TPO to be generally effective, it must exhibit the following characteristics:
- A high profile in the location and physical design of office, presentation of information and marketing collateral;
- A clear marketing plan with a targeting strategy based on a sectoral approach;
- A proactive stance in identifying and making contact with potential customers;
- Sufficient numbers of staff with appropriate skills.

For a TPO to be able to provide support for the SME sector, additionally it has to:
- Identify a match between the capabilities of SMEs and the requirements of customers in terms of price and quality, volume, delivery and distribution;
- Identify opportunities for sub-contracting linkages and for clusters of SMEs, as opposed to individual firms, to fulfil customer requirements;
- Disseminate information in a way that is easy for SMEs to access and understand.

MEDIA has representation in a number of export markets. However, it fails to exploit TPOs sufficiently for the following reasons:
- The distribution of overseas offices and representatives falls short of creating a significant presence in key OECD markets, such as the US, the EU and Japan;
- One-person offices are unable to engage in the required range of activities, or the type of proactive results-driven direct marketing;
- TPOs are not sufficiently integrated into the overall strategy of MEDIA.
- TPOs take little account of the SME sector.

TPOs represent a highly cost-effective mechanism for entering and penetrating overseas markets and should be given greater importance in MEDIA's future plans.

Box 4 – The Business Link

The proposed Business Link is adapted from the model established and operating effectively in the UK. The key elements of the concept are as follows:
- The principle purpose of the Business Link is to address the major factor of small business failure – weakness in management skills. The Business Link acts as a hub providing information and advice in all areas of the SME's operation, addressing both its external and internal environments. It is primarily targeted at established businesses with clearly identifiable growth potential, but can also direct start-ups and micro-businesses to appropriate assistance and advice.
- The Business Link operates as a professional, client-centred business offering a range of tailored services, adopting a culture of high quality, and monitoring and evaluating the effectiveness of its overall service and individual service offers on a regular basis. All advice offered by the Business Link is independent and objective, and tailored directly to the individual needs of its clients.
- Although not seeking to maximise profit, the Business Link is a commercial body with a public purpose. It is funded partly from public sources and partly from client fees. It is accountable to all of its stakeholders for the quality and effectiveness of its provision.
- The Business Link works together with partners in both the public and private sectors to foster an integrated approach to service delivery. It utilises

existing, effective service provision, where appropriate. It also acts as a catalyst for the development of a network of service suppliers, thus creating the demand for a new sub-sector of independent small businesses.

- The Business Link employs only staff of the highest calibre in order to deliver the highest possible quality of service and to ensure the level of credibility needed for it to be effective in its own marketplace.

The Business Link offers the following core services:

Gateway Service – the first point of contact with the customer and a means of determining the nature of the support that the customer requires.

Information Service – provides customers with access to desk research and business intelligence, primarily through on-line databases.

Business Library – a dedicated Business Link library offering a comprehensive and up-to-date range of resource materials, supplemented by links with other libraries, e.g. university, public libraries, etc.

The Personal Business Advisor – at the heart of the Business Link concept, the PBA's fundamental role is to develop relationships with a select number of established businesses in order to help them realise growth. Elements of this role include assessing the needs of clients and directing them to appropriate service providers, managing the relationship over time, and monitoring results. Ideally, PBA's should have skills and knowledge that are appropriate to their clients.

Specialist advisors – These may be divided into a number of categories, for example: design, innovation and technology, international trade, finance, management, training and human resources, marketing, premises and planning, regulatory issues, supply chain development. These specialist advisors may be directly employed by Business Link, or as appropriate, be private sector organisations working in partnership with the Business Link.

Start-up and micro-business services – whilst the PBAs and other resource-intensive services are targeted at firms with clearly identifiable growth potential, the Business Link can direct start-ups or micro-businesses to specific assistance delivered by a specialist organisation.

Figure A.3: A Business Link for Mauritius

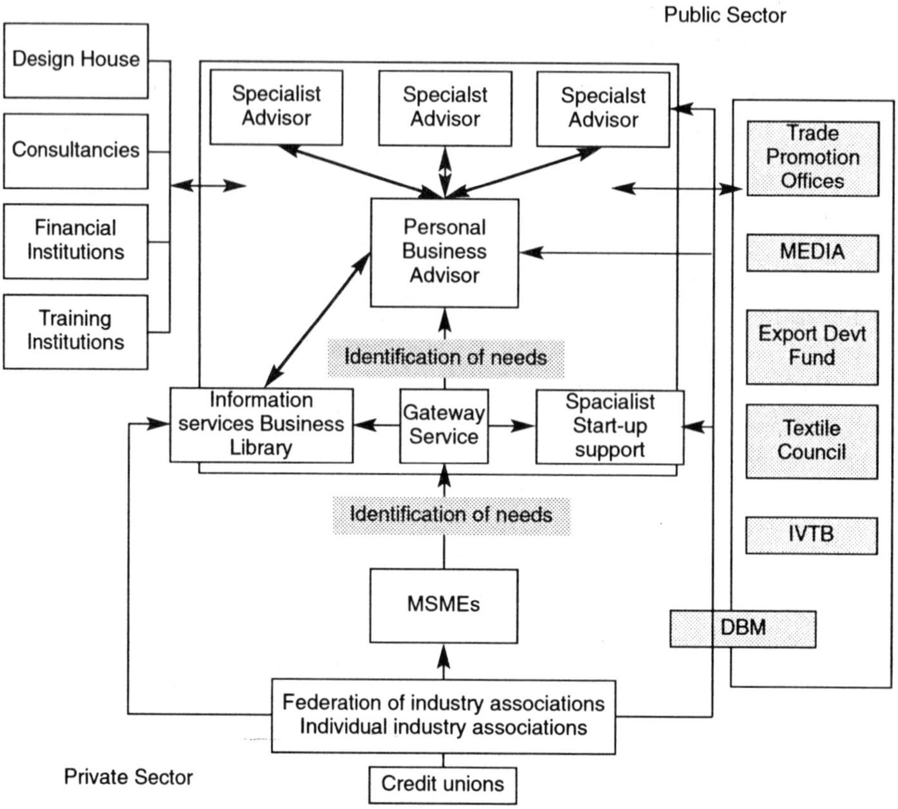

Public Sector

- Design House
- Consultancies
- Financial Institutions
- Training Institutions

- Specialist Advisor
- Specialst Advisor
- Specialst Advisor

- Personal Business Advisor

Identification of needs

- Information services Business Library
- Gateway Service
- Spacialist Start-up support

Identification of needs

MSMEs

Federation of industry associations
Individual industry associations

Credit unions

Private Sector

- Trade Promotion Offices
- MEDIA
- Export Devt Fund
- Textile Council
- IVTB
- DBM

Box 5 – The Design House – Infusing Design Culture into Mauritius

The Design House is, literally, a building containing a number of studio apartments with workshops attached, ideally located near a beach. The design of the building itself should reflect its purpose: it should look attractive and approachable and embody good architectural design.

The aim is to fill the apartments with practitioners of different design disciplines. These might include:

- Product design
- Graphic design
- Fashion design
- Shoe design

- Interior design
- Jewellery design
- Fabric design
- Furniture design

The apartments would be offered to young designers primarily from Europe, the US and Japan. The designers need to be formally qualified and have at least two years' commercial experience. Contracts would be for one year, renewable for an additional year only, so as to ensure a constant supply of new thinking and approaches.

Designers would be expected to earn their living through a combination of teaching at Mauritian educational institutions, providing design consultancy to businesses, and running private short courses at their workshops. Design consultancy provided to SMEs would be engineered by the Business Link and partially state funded. Designers could contribute to policy-making by the Design Council, offer support to industry associations and make significant contributions to government organisations and initiatives such as Mauritius Week. They might also be able to continue with consultancy projects from their home country.

Designers would not be expected to pay rent, but would be obliged to take on an apprentice for one year. This apprenticeship could form part of a formal qualification in the relevant design discipline, if such a course is offered in Mauritius. The apprentice might be funded by the state.

It is envisaged that the proposition would appeal mostly to younger designers, whose personal circumstances would allow them the time, and who would be attracted by the novelty, the challenge and the location.

The benefits to Mauritius are many. The range of design disciplines would enable most businesses to access a relevant designer and could create the impetus for the development of new businesses. The cumulative effect of so much design input, with each designer spawning another, would enable Mauritius to build its design capability within a very short time.

Initiatives with similar objectives, but different forms of implementation, are successfully running in transition economies, notably Romania and Poland.

Box 6 – The Clothes Shop and Sample Library: Simulating Conditions in Sophisticated Export Markets

For Mauritians with little or no personal exposure to overseas markets, especially with developed countries, it is very difficult to gauge the level or nature of quality that would be competitive in those markets.

For example, in the textile industry, for example, there is no substitute for one's own senses: seeing, hearing and feeling the cut of a jacket, the feel of the cloth, the colour of the fabric, the way clothes are presented in the shop, or the appearance of the shop itself.

Whilst it is always preferable to provide opportunities for Mauritians to travel to overseas markets, a cost-effective way to bring the markets for textiles to Mauritius is to create a clothes shop on the island.

It is envisaged that, within the Clothing Technology Centre, a shop is built which, in its interior design, merchandising and stock selection, would simulate an upmarket retail outlet in, say, London, Paris or New York. Stock would be sourced from world-class manufacturers, ideally on a donation basis, and renewed each season.

The nature of the shop would rotate on a regular basis. So, for example, for two months the shop would be for ladieswear, the next two months for menswear, afterwards for childrenswear, then shoes and so on. To enable this rotation, the interior fittings and merchandise fixtures would need to be flexible.

To supplement this shop, a library of clothing samples would house a much larger range of clothing, as well as the current season's clothing not displayed.

The Textile Council would manage this initiative with input from the Design House.

Box 7 – SME Clusters: Leveraging Collective Efficiency

There is mounting evidence that clustering and networking help small firms to compete and grow. By working together, firms can gain the benefits of collective efficiency, enabling them to challenge larger competitors and break into national and global markets.1

Clusters refer to the sectoral and geographic concentration of firms, leading to incidental benefits in terms of finding suppliers, customers, skilled workers, etc. These are often referred to as industrial districts, well-known examples are to be found in Northern Italy.

Networks refer to cases of inter-firm co-operation irrespective of whether firms are geographically close. Here joint action is consciously pursued, in the form of co-operation between individual firms or groups of firms joining together in business associations and producer consortia.

The principles of collective efficiency, as suggested by Hubert Schmitz in the study noted above, are a 'Triple C' approach – a *customer-orientation* which forces firms to tackle the key problems of competitiveness; a *collective approach* which builds on the formation of groups of firms, associations, etc; and the *cumulative capacity* to upgrade through continuous improvement and, over time, to become less dependent on support from outside.

Whether or not clusters already exist, networks pursuing conscious joint action can be stimulated through appropriate state interventions. Examples cited by Schmitz include:

Woodworking in the Brazilian State of Ceará. The Brazilian SME promotion agency, SEBRAE, channelled a government contract for school furniture to a group of small firms in one two. Their industry association engineered the bid and the co-ordination of contracts. Individual firms formed teams to discuss customer needs, technical, production and other issues. In this way, small firms began to develop a customer-orientation. SEBRAE provided additional training where needed, thus enabling the sector to develop its own impetus and processes for further development. The impact on the town was impressive. Before the contract there were four sawmills with 12 employees. Five years later, there were 42 sawmills with about 350 workers and a further 1,000 people employed in the woodworking industry. Over time, the customer base has been extended, so that 70% of output now goes to the private sector.

Surgical instrument-making in Pakistan. The town of Sialkot in Pakistan produces scissors, forceps and a whole range of specialist precision instruments. They are made from high-grade stainless steel by over 300 manufacturers, who farm out work to another 1,500 small enterprises specialising in particular stages of the production process. Alongside these firms, there are an estimated 200 suppliers of inputs and over 800 units providing various types of services. Over 90% of Sialkot's output is exported, most of it to Europe and North America. Overall, it is estimated that the cluster accounts for 20% of world exports, making Pakistan (after Germany) the second largest exporter of surgical instruments.

Box 8 – Export Houses and Export Consultancies: Creating Specialisms in the Private Sector

Two concepts underpin this proposal. The first is that one of the major barriers to SME growth is the difficulty in identifying potential export markets. Few SMEs have the resources, time and skills, to conduct comprehensive market scanning activities, or the funds to engage specialists. Even if export markets are identified, further difficulties exist in getting close enough to potential customers to know their needs and how they can be satisfied in designing and developing products and services. Yet another hurdle for SMEs is entering new export markets: making contacts with individual customers, understanding and negotiating factors within the macro-environment.

The second underpinning concept is that government-funded business development services need to become more business-like; deliver products or services tailored, usually on a sectoral basis, to individual SMEs; and foster sustainable development, where assistance becomes finite. Increasingly, the idea of subsidiarity is emerging in the literature1. This means that the provision of SME support services should be delegated to the lowest possible level of those who are closest to the SME sector, thus engendering a degree of "ownership".

It is not the role of the Business Link directly to find new markets for SMEs or to facilitate their entry into these markets. Encouraging the emergence of private sector export houses and export consultancies, at the same time addresses one of the major barriers to SME growth and also creates the demand for a new SME sector. The Business Link might purchase, or part-purchase, services on behalf of SMEs as part of a financial support package on a commercial contract basis. Any firm, SME or larger, could use the services of these suppliers as and when required on a fee basis.

Export consultancies are likely to specialise in a geographic market, with a cross-specialisation in a limited number of products. So, for example, a consultancy in Mauritius might build expertise in textiles to the European Union, or food products to the African mainland. Consultancies would provide advice and information on conditions within a given export market, factors relating to market entry, competitor analysis and possibly the identification of customer groups. The Competitiveness Council, or other government organisation, could commission export consultancies to produce industry- or market-specific opportunity analysis reports.

Export houses act as extensions of an SME's marketing capability, contracting to enter an export market on behalf of one individual firm or a group of firms. Export houses might undertake the initial research, make contact and negotiate with customers, or formulate contracts. They would have the required knowledge to make significant contributions to new product or service development. As with export consultancies, these houses would be most effective if they were to specialise by product/market. Export houses could be remunerated on a fee or commission basis, or a combination of these.

It is likely that export consultancies would set up departments to act as export houses, or vice versa. The expertise gained within the consultancy is, in itself, a saleable export.

Bibliography

Aaby, N.E and Slater, S.F(1989), "Marketing Influences on Export Performance: A Review of the Empirical Literature, 1978- 88", *International Marketing Review*, Vol.6 No.4.

Albaum, G. et al (1994), *International Marketing and Export Management*, London, Addison-Wesley Publishing Company

Appanah, V. (1997), *The Challenge of Productivity*, Port Louis, Edition Ocean Indien

Autio, E., and Klofsten, M. (1998), 'A Comparative Study of Two European Business Incubators, *Journal of Small Business Management*, Vol. 36. No. 1

Badrinath, R. (1994), 'Helping Small and Medium-Size Firms to Enter Export Markets', Geneva, *International Trade Forum*

Bagnasco, A., and Sabel, C. (Eds) (1995), *Small and Medium-Size Enterprises*, London, Cassell

Bank of Mauritius (1997), *Annual Report: Year Ended 30th June 1997*, Port Louis: Bank of Mauritius.

Bannock, G. et al (1987), *Into Active Exporting*, London, British Overseas Trade Board

Barber, J. et al (Eds) (1992), *Barriers to Growth in Small Firms*, London, Routledge

Bilkey, W. J., and Tesar, G. (1977), "The Export Behaviour of Smaller-sized Wisconsin Manufacturing Firms", *Journal of International Business Studies*, Vol. 8, No. 1

Birchall, D. W., Chanaron, J. J., and Soderquist, K. (1996), 'Managing innovation in SMEs: a comparison of companies in the UK, France and Portugal, *International Journal of Technology Management*, Vol. 12, No. 3

Buckley, P., Campos, J., Mirza, H, and White, E. (1997), *International Technology Transfer By Small and Medium-Sized Enterprises*, London: Macmillan Press.

Business Link (1997), *Service Guide No. 3*, London: Department of Trade and Industry.

Cafferata, R., and Mensi, R. (1995), The Role of Information in the Internationalisation of SMEs: A Typological Approach, *International Small Business Journal*, Vol. 13, No. 3

Central Statistical Office (1994), 1992 *Census of Economic Activities: Vol. 1 Small Establishments and Itinerant Units*, Port Louis: Ministry of Economic Planning and Development.

Central Statistical Office (1997), *Annual Digest of Statistics 1996*, Port Louis: Ministry of Economic Planning and Development.

Chetty, S. K., and Hamilton, R. T. (1996) 'The Process of Exporting in Owner-controlled Firms' *International Small Business Journal*, Vol. 14, No. 2

Commonwealth Secretariat (1998) *An Integrated Marketing Programme for the Mauritian Printing and Publishing Sector, Part1: An overview of the Mauritian Printing Industry*, prepared by J. Birkenshaw and C. Johnston, London: Commonwealth Secretariat.

Curran, J., and Blackburn, R. (1994), *Small Firms and Local Economic Networks*, London: Chapman Publishing Ltd.

Dawson, J. (1997), 'Beyond Credit – the Emergence of High-Impact, Cost-Effective Business Development Services, *Small Enterprise Development*, Vol. 8, No. 3

DBM (1998) *Annual Report*, Port Louis: Development Bank of Mauritius.

De Chazal Du Mee (1998), "Research Study on Small and Medium Enterprises: First Interim Report", Port Louis: De Chazal Du Mee.

Dichtl, E., Koegimayr, H., and Mueller, S. (1990), 'International Orientations as a Precondition for Export Success', *Journal of International Business Studies*, Vol. 21, No. 1

DTI (1996), *Small Firms in Britain: Report 1996*, London: Department of Trade and Industry.

Dubois, P. R., Beedasy, J., Hurreeram, D. K., Ramgutty-Wong, A., and Seebaluck, D. (1996), *Technological Competence in Mauritian Small and Medium Enterprises*, Port Louis: University of Mauritius.

EIU (1998), *EIU Country Report: Mauritius, 4th Quarter 1998*, London: Economic Intelligence Unit.

EPZDA (1998) *Annual Report*, Port Louis: Export Processing Zone Development Authority.

EPZDA (1999), "Report of Task Force on Textiles", Port Louis: Export Processing Zone Development Authority

Gantisky, J. (1989), "Strategies for Innate and Adoptive Exporters: Lessons from Israel's Case, *International Marketing Review*, Vol. 6, No. 5

Gibson, A. (1997), 'Business Development Services: Core Principles and Future Challenges', *Small Enterprise Development*, Vol. 8, No. 3

Global Financial Services Ltd (undated), "Draft Preliminary Report on Venture Capital Fund and Mutual Guarantee Fund for Small and Medium-Sized Enterprises" Prepared for the European Union Delegation of the European Commission.

Goss, D., and Jones, R. (1992), Organisation Structure and SME Training Provision, *International Small Business Journal*, Vol. 10, No. 4

Greiner, L. (1972), "Evolution and Revolution as Organizations Grow", *Harvard Business Review*, July/August

Hall, G. (1995), *Surviving and Prospering in the Small Firm Sector*, London: Routledge.

Hofstede, G. (1980), *Culture's Consequences*, London: Sage

Humphrey, J., and Schmitz, H. (1996), "The Triple C Approach to Local Industrial Policy", *World Development*, Vol.24, No.12

JEC (1998), "Memorandum of the JEC on 1998/99 Budget", Port Louis: Joint Economic Council (cited as JEC in the text).

Jeetun, A. (1997), "Policy Coherence and Small Enterprise Development", Port Louis: Mauritius Employers Federation, (unpublished).

Jennings, P., and Beaver, G. (1997), "The Performance and Competitive Advantage of Small Firms: A Management Perspective", *International Small Business Journal*, Vol. 15, No. 2

Katsikeas, C. S., Al-Khalifa, A., and Crick, D. (1997) "Manufacturers' Understanding of their Overseas Distributors: the Relevance of Export Involvement" *International Business Review*, Vol. 6, No. 2

Kuada, J. (1997), "Export Motives and Strategies of Ghanaian Firms", Paper presented at the *Sixth International Conference on Marketing and Development*, Romania

Lall, S., and Wignaraja, G. (1998), *Mauritius: Dynamising Export Competitiveness*, Commonwealth Economic Paper No 33, London: Commonwealth Secretariat.

Little, I., Mazumdar, D., and Page, J. (1987), *Small Manufacturing Enterprises: A Comparative Analysis of India and Other Economies*, Oxford: Oxford University Press.

Louter, P. J., Ouwerkerk, C., and Bakker, B. A. (1991)"An Inquiry into Successful Exporting", *European Journal of Marketing*, Vol. 24, No. 6

Malhotra, V. (1994), "Programme for Development of Small Scale Industries in Mauritius", Vienna: UNIDO.

Manu, G. (1998), 'Enterprise Development in Africa – Strategies for Impact and Growth', *Small Enterprise Development*, Vol. 9, No. 4

MCCI (1998), *Annual Report 1997*, Port Louis: Mauritius Chamber of Commerce & Industry.

Mead, D.C and Liedholm, C. (1998), "The Dynamics of Micro and Small Enterprises in Developing Countries", *World Development*, Vol. 26, No. 1

MEDIA (1998) *Annual Report*, Port Louis: Mauritius Export Development and Investment Authority.

MEDRC (1997), Vision 2020: *The National Long-Term Perspective Study*, Vol. 1 and 2, Port Louis: Ministry of Economic Development and Regional Co-operation.

MEF (1998), *Annual Report 1997*, Port Louis: Mauritius Employers Federation.

Meier, R. and Pilgrim, M. (1994), "Policy Induced Constraints on Small Enterprise Development in Asian Developing Countries", *Small Enterprise Development*, Vol. 5, No. 1

Mendonca, M., and Kanungo, R. N. (1996), 'Impact of culture on performance management in developing countries', *International Journal of Manpower*, Vol. 17, No. 4/5

Milner, C., and McKay, A. (1996), 'Real Exchange Rate Measures of Trade Liberalisation: Some Evidence for Mauritius', *Journal of African Economies*, Vol. 5, No. 1

Ministry of Industry and Commerce (1998), *The One Stop Shop*, Port Louis: Ministry of Industry and Commerce.

Moran, P. (1998), 'Personality Characteristics and Growth-orientation of the Small Business Owner-manager', *International Small Business Journal*, Vol. 16, No. 3

MOIC (1997), "Enhancing the Competitiveness of the SME Sector: Project Proposal for Financing by the European Union", Prepared by the Ministry of Industry and Commerce, Mauritius.

Murphy, D. and Suttle, A. (1998), "Study on the Activities of MEDIA" Dublin: International Development Ireland Ltd.

Nadvi, K. (1998), 'International Competitiveness and Small Firm Clusters – Evidence from Pakistan', *Small Enterprise Development*, Vol. 9, No. 1

Philp, N. E. (1998), 'The Export Propensity of the Very Small Enterprise (VSE)', *International Small Business Journal*, Vol.16, No. 4

Porter M, (1980), *Competitive Strategy*, New York: Free Press

Rabellotti, R. (1998), 'Helping Small Firms to Network – the Experience of UNIDO', *Small Enterprise Development*, Vol. 9, No. 1

Schmitz, H. (1998), 'Fostering Collective Efficiency', *Small Enterprise Development*, Vol. 9, No. 1

Sengenberger, W., Loveman, G.W. and Piore, M.J. (ed. 1990), *The Re-Emergence of Small Enterprises: Industrial Restructuring in Industrialised Countries*, Geneva: International Institute for Labour Studies.

Shoham, A. and Albaum, G. (1995), 'Reducing the Impact of Barriers to Exporting: A Managerial Perspective', *Journal of International Marketing*, Vol. 3, No. 4.

SMIDO (1996), *A New Vision for SME Development*, Coromandel: SMIDO.

SMIDO (1998) Annual Report, Coromandel: SMIDO.

Srinivas, K. M. (1995), 'Globalization of Business and the Third World: Challenge of expanding the mindsets', *Journal of Management Development*, Vol. 14. No. 3

SSEAM (1998), "Memorandum to the Minster of Finance", Small Scale Entrepreneur Association of Mauritius (Cited as SSEAM in the text).

Storey, D. (1994), *Understanding the Small Business Sector*, London: Routledge

Theng, L. G. and Lim Wang Boon, J. (1997), "An Exploratory Study of Factors Affecting the Failure of Local Small and Medium Enterprises", *Asia Pacific Journal of Management*, Vol. 13, No. 2

UN (1998), World Investment Report 1998, New York: United Nations.

Wignaraja, G. (1997), "Manufacturing Competitiveness With Special Reference to Small States" in Commonwealth Secretariat, *Small States: Economic Review and Basic Statistics*, London: Commonwealth Secretariat.

Wignaraja, G. (1998), *Trade Liberalisation in Sri Lanka: Exports, Technology and Industrial Policy*, London: Macmillan.

Wignaraja, G. (1999), "Tackling National Competitiveness in a Borderless World", *Commonwealth Business Council Policy Paper Series No.1*.

Woldekidan, B. (1994), *Export-led Growth in Mauritius*, Indian Ocean Policy Paper 3, National Centre for Development Studies, Canberra: Australian National University.

World Trade Organisation (1996), *Trade Policy Review: Mauritius 1995*, Geneva: World Trade Organisation.

World Bank (1994.a), *Mauritius: Technology Strategy for Competitiveness*, Report No. 12518-MAS, Washington DC: World Bank.

World Bank (1998), *World Development Report 1998*, Oxford: Oxford University Press.

World Bank (1998a), *World Development Indicators 1998*, Oxford: Oxford University Press.

Wren, B. M., Simpson J. T. and Paul, C. (1998), 'Marketing Channel Relationships Among Small Businesses' *International Small Business Journal*, Vol. 16. No. 4

Yeoh, P-L. and Jeong, I. (1995), 'Contingency relationships between entrepreneurship, export channel structure and environment' *European Journal of Marketing*, Vol. 29, No. 8.